Discover Your Unknown Inner Self

A Pathway to Wisdom and Wholeness

EMILY WELLS

BALBOA.
PRESS

A DIVISION OF HAY HOUSE

The information, ideas, and suggestions in this book are not intended as a substitute for professional medical advice. Before following any suggestions contained in this book, you should consult your personal physician. Neither the author nor the publisher shall be liable or responsible for any loss or damage allegedly arising as a consequence of your use or application of any information or suggestions in this book.

Balboa Press books may be ordered through booksellers or by contacting:

Balboa Press
A Division of Hay House
1663 Liberty Drive
Bloomington, IN 47403
www.balboapress.com
1 (877) 407-4847

Because of the dynamic nature of the Internet, any web addresses or links contained in this book may have changed since publication and may no longer be valid. The views expressed in this work are solely those of the author and do not necessarily reflect the views of the publisher, and the publisher hereby disclaims any responsibility for them.

The author of this book does not dispense medical advice or prescribe the use of any technique as a form of treatment for physical, emotional, or medical problems without the advice of a physician, either directly or indirectly. The intent of the author is only to offer information of a general nature to help you in your quest for emotional and spiritual well-being. In the event you use any of the information in this book for yourself, which is your constitutional right, the author and the publisher assume no responsibility for your actions.

Print information available on the last page.

ISBN: 978-1-9822-1881-2 (sc)
ISBN: 978-1-9822-1879-9 (hc)
ISBN: 978-1-9822-1880-5 (e)

Library of Congress Control Number: 2018915158

Balboa Press rev. date: 02/26/2019

I dedicate this book to Georgie and my inner children,
who helped me both to begin and to walk this amazing journey.

Contents

Foreword

It has been my deep pleasure to know Emily Wells for twenty-plus years. She was a member of my congregation when I served the Unity Church in Salem, Oregon. In March 2012, Emily asked if I would do some inner-child work with her. That request started both of us on an incredible journey into Emily's inner self. Although Emily did all the work, she graciously allowed me to walk along and offer her a little guidance here and there. I have seldom worked with anyone who has been so devoted to her internal journey. From the first week, Emily was committed to a schedule of weekly sessions, spending every Monday in dialogue with her internal aspects. In the process, she learned more and more of who she is, and she came to understand and heal the events that shaped her life, some of which caused her pain and some of which contributed to her courage, strength, and commitment. Although I have worked with a number of people on inner-child spiritual work as a minister, I have never seen anyone uncover and develop his or her internal aspects as Emily has. Her book gives us a model to follow and a light of hope to reach for as we open to our unknown inner selves. Thank you, Emily, for having the commitment and courage to share your story with all of us.

Reverend Georgie Richardson

Acknowledgments

GEORGIE RICHARDSON, WHO SUPPORTED me on this journey every step of the way and believed in me long before I could believe in myself.

Michael Hoefler and Joan M., who helped in countless ways, especially in knowing that what was happening to me was real and assisting me in walking my chosen path.

Alandra N. Kai, Marisa M., and my inner children, who gave me the reason to begin the journey.

Sonia Choquette, Jean Haner, and Cynthia Slon, who helped me see the big picture along the way.

Suzanne Ward (the Matthew Books series), who helped me understand that what was happening to me was real and edited the beginning and ending of this book.

Qigong Master Chunyi Lin and Ani Avedissian for healing assistance before and during the publishing process.

Mary Jo Wevers for astrological assistance and encouragement.

Eileen Sakai and Barb Vandepas, who gave invaluable feedback and encouragement throughout the publishing process.

Faye Boyd-Wright, Katherine Hancock, Roxanne Hanneman, Tonya Jefferies, Ellen Langsather, April Loop, Catherine Tomich Luthe, Joanie Manuel, Molly Murphy, Karen O'Neill, Sue Reiley, Ani Remme, Lorena Smith, Malia Ladd, Annie Thorp, Denita Wallace, Edward Wickwire, and Kristen Wilson, who listened to my words and gave encouragement.

Susie Young, Sue Short, and Christine Shephard for computer assistance.

Mary Ramirez, Victoria Goodwin, and all the others from Balboa Press for assistance in the publishing process.

All those who attended the first Inner-Team workshop for participation in something new and unique.

My support team, my aspects, my higher self, my soul, my body, my dreams, and all parts of myself who made this journey possible.

All others who shared their love and support with me in countless ways through the space of this journey.

I give heartfelt love, gratitude, and blessings to all of the above.

Introduction

THE BOOK YOU ARE about to read is true and relayed exactly as each event occurred. I don't know why any of this happened to me; I just know that it did, and it turned out to be a life-changing journey.

When it began, I had no idea where it was leading—I simply followed, one step at a time, a path that unfolded before me. Often, I was completely amazed and would pause and say to myself, "This must be real, as I couldn't possibly be making it up!"

I explored unknown paths within myself and discovered parts that I came to call my aspects. These aspects, with whom I had revealing dialogues, had great wisdom and love for me. My experience with them became transformative, and like most transformations, it was sometimes raw and uncomfortable. Other times, it was so filled with love that I wept.

I invite you to join me as I share my exploration into the unknown through these intimate dialogues, which are completely uncensored and straight from my heart. Even though this information is deeply personal, it longs to be shared with others. I cannot explain this. Possibly we are all connected on some level, and maybe my experience will inspire you to explore within your own self to see what wisdom awaits discovery.

Chapter 1

Life-Changing Journey Begins

FEAR STRUCK AS I heard the following: "This summer, you might experience some health challenges, but you have nothing to fear. You will get through this. You just need to relax. You will be all right." Relaxing was the last thing I could do after hearing those words from a gifted intuitive in January 2012.

Five years previously, I'd been treated for breast cancer, so fear around any mention of health issues was an automatic reaction. At the end of March 2012, my anxiety led me to a medical intuitive, who told me that if I did inner-child work, I could avoid all health issues.

My life-changing journey began. I made an appointment with Georgie, a spiritual counselor who had assisted many others in their inner-child work.

The night before my first appointment with Georgie, I had an unusual dream I called Prisoner. I was a prisoner in a camp where the guards were called Rigid Taskmaster and Stern Enforcer. When

I was allowed to leave, they warned me, "It is very dangerous out there."

April 7, 2012

I have my first session with Georgie. When I tell her about the unusual dream, she says the dream aspects have been with me for a long time and have a purpose and gifts to share. She suggests I investigate this.

April 24, 2012

Intrigued, I accept her suggestion. I sit quietly alone, and in my mind, I ask Rigid Taskmaster and Stern Enforcer if they have anything to share with me.

I am so surprised to see images of them in my mind's eye and hear them speak that I am not prepared to record their words, but I remember them: "We are your protectors. You were too frightened to take on the role of keeping yourself safe. We are freeing you."

RIGID TASKMASTER. I am the one who helps you get something done with determination and commitment. I am tenacity.

STERN ENFORCER. I am the one who gives you the push to get something done. I am courage.

May 3, 2012

I meet with Georgie and share my first dialogue. We decide I have contacted aspects of myself who have a positive reason for staying with me, and I am forming a team. She suggests I learn about these positive reasons.

May 8, 2012

Bubbling with curiosity and apprehension, I sit alone and ask Rigid Taskmaster and Stern Enforcer if they have a positive reason for being with me. I hear Rigid Taskmaster say, "I am tenacity," and Stern Enforcer says, "I am courage." I welcome the first two members of the team and begin my inner exploration.

I diligently go through John Bradshaw's book *Homecoming: Reclaiming and Championing Your Inner Child*, completing each exercise and doing each meditation. I am determined to avoid health issues, and I'm willing to do my part. In the process, I uncover many flawed core beliefs and a whole range of dysfunctional family roles. Then I have another curious dream.

May 10, 2012

I call this dream Saboteur. In it, I am interrupted as I watch the performance of a group I've been coaching. I am told there are plastic jacks and small toy cars left on the stairs leading up to the main office. I know this is dangerous, as someone could step on the objects, trip, and fall, so I leave the performance. As I pick up the objects, I realize they were placed on purpose; this is no accident. I am awake enough to ask who put the jacks on the stairs, and the word *saboteur* forms in my mind. I also see in my mind's eye a slender, dark, slinky figure hiding upstairs.

June 4, 2012

I build up the courage to try my first written dialogue. I sit alone with my notebook and pen and bring the dream image of Saboteur into my mind.

There is no how-to book for what I do next. I am led solely by my own inner direction.

My first written dialogue unfolds as follows:

EMILY. I would like to talk with my saboteur part, who is now hiding in a small space. I see your slim, elongated body dressed in black. Would you please come out today? I can feel your fear and pain. I'm here for you. I do not judge you for leaving the jacks and toy cars on the steps to trip people up. I thank you for revealing yourself. I see you standing out of the crack in the wall now. Do you have a message for me?

SABOTEUR. I hate being me. I hate who I am. I hate this life I am leading. I want it to change. At one time, I wanted it to end. Yes, I am afraid, and yes, I am in a lot of pain. I do not believe you can do anything to help. This is the way our life has always been. It will not change. You cannot help me. It is hopeless.

Moved with great compassion for this sad part of myself, I ask a question without thinking.

EMILY. Will you at least let me hold you? I feel your fear, pain, anger, frustration, and hopelessness. I cannot promise anything, but I can love you.

Saboteur moves in front of my heart, and I hold the imaginary figure in my real physical arms.

EMILY. It is all right to feel the way you do. I still love you anyway! Let's start with fear.

It comes to me to release this fear, and I make a sound of fear—a high-pitched *eeeeee*. I sit rocking back and forth, holding and loving my saboteur image. I add emotional freedom technique (EFT) tapping to the process. After a few minutes, I feel that the fear and pain seem to be gone for now, and Saboteur has relaxed some in my arms.

EMILY. Ready to release anger? No? All right we will do hopelessness.

I make a low rumbling *ooooooo* sound from my chest. I feel despair, and my arms go weak. I rock back and forth and do EFT tapping. Again, in a few minutes, I feel better.

EMILY. Oh, Saboteur, I love you. You are so sad. You have been with me so long. You have tried hard to help me. I love you. I appreciate you. Do you have another name I could call you as your positive reason for being with me?

I try the words *careful, cautious, worthy,* and *flexible* in my mind, but nothing feels definite.

EMILY. Thank you anyway. Are you ready for anger now? Yes.

I make a loud, angry *arrrrrr* sound from my abdomen and continue the EFT tapping and rocking until I feel better.

EMILY. I see you have a black-and-white-striped outfit. This is a step up from all black. I am pleased to see this. I see you now moving to yellow and black stripes. And you like the name Flexible? Try it on for a while, and see how it feels. I see a smile on your face. Yes? Do you have anything to say?

FLEXIBLE. I feel much better. I'm glad you came for me. I want to be with you.

EMILY. I love you. Would like you to be on the team?

I hear nothing.

All of the dialogues in this book happen inside my head, but I physically do the processes. I feel a shift in my energy field as each one occurs. I have never experienced anything like this before, but it feels beneficial, so I continue.

5

June 5, 2012

I meet with Georgie and share the above experience as well as the results from my inner-child exercises in which I identified a flawed core belief that I am defective.

I also share the results of an astrology chart interpretation I recently had with Mary Jo Wevers, Jungian karmic astrologer. I had never thought of having an astrology reading before, but the urge to have one was strong, and I acted upon it. To my amazement, through this interpretation, my challenging life suddenly made sense for the first time.

June 12, 2012

I sit alone, ready to write, with the hope that I will be able to dialogue with this defective part of myself. I can hardly believe what happened the other time I tried this, but I'm determined to avoid health issues and curious to learn more about these hidden parts of myself, so I begin. To my surprise, the following dialogue transpires in my mind:

EMILY. I am open to a dialogue with my part called Defective, the one who says there is something wrong with me. Please reply.

DEFECTIVE. Of course there is something wrong with you. Just look at your life; look at your relationships. You have no idea how to have joy and play, at least at this time and at most times in the past. Of course I am here, and I am not leaving.

EMILY. Why are you here?

DEFECTIVE. It is obvious. You will get too proud and misuse your power just like the astrology reading said. It is true. You chose this low self-esteem life to redeem yourself, so I am staying for your own good.

EMILY. Amazing! I am grateful to you. I can hardly believe we are having this talk at exactly the perfect time for me to really hear you. What if I told you I am now ready to acknowledge the truth that you speak of and to make amends?

I recently learned about this situation from my astrology reading, and I am doing a process to release and forgive the event.

DEFECTIVE. I will believe it when I see it, but I want you to know I will support you in this plan. I will not block your efforts. When you are complete, I will be here to resume this conversation. In fact, I applaud your getting this far.

EMILY. Thank you very much, and thanks for your clarity.

I now have a list of flawed core beliefs from my inner-child process. Since this worked with Defective, I am prompted to try a dialogue with Unlovable. Here is the result:

EMILY. I am now ready to open a dialogue with my unlovable part. I feel your presence inside.

I hear nothing, but I sense some words and hold a monologue in my mind.

EMILY. You are preverbal and very deep? Maybe there is an aspect of this part who is willing to speak with me? Maybe you are not preverbal, but you are not ready to speak with me? You are buried very deep inside? It is safe to come out now. I have already called in all the angels, God, Jesus, my higher self, and holy ones to help us. You began before I was born? You began in utero—this fear of not being loved?

At last, I hear these words:

UNLOVABLE. Once again, this was something you chose to do in this lifetime.

My throat is tight, and I am tense, but I persevere. I find this amazing and must follow where I am being led.

EMILY. Thank you for speaking. Please continue.

UNLOVABLE. Oh, I am here all right, and I am holding on tightly. That is why you are feeling a tight throat and chest. Keep breathing and tapping. You do not have to fear me. I am here for a huge purpose. You wanted to fully experience God's love and the love of others in this life. You could not have had this experience if you felt their love all along. Relax into the idea of being loved. This is not a matter of just changing my name. You must allow God's love. It is eternal. It has always been here and always will be.

EMILY. How do I do this? Can you help me?

UNLOVABLE. First, you need to change my name.

EMILY. All right.

I smile, and the words *precious* and *beloved* come to me. I hear the following:

UNLOVABLE. Precious belongs to Unworthy. I am Beloved!

EMILY. Unbelievable! Please help me to believe that this is real.

BELOVED. Feel my presence. Just feel. Feel the sadness, the pain, the fear—the fear of this not being real. Oh, but I am real. I am Beloved, and you are beloved. Let out the sadness. Let out the fear. Make your release sounds.

Tears flow, and I make my sad sounds.

EMILY. Oh yes, that helps. Thank you.

BELOVED. Now feel my presence surrounding you. Feel my presence within you. This is my love. Allow me to merge with you when you are ready. There is no rush. Just allow.

EMILY. I am trying. I feel nothing.

BELOVED. Just know that I am here. When you are ready, we will merge. There is no hurry. I will never leave you.

EMILY. Thank you. I feel unworthy.

BELOVED. I know you do. Do not rush. This process is all in divine order. Just relax and allow. It is time to rest.

EMILY. Thank you. Thank you. Thank you. I am overflowing with gratitude!

I close my second day of written dialogues and one of the most amazing experiences in my life. I know I cannot possibly be making this up, as I have no idea what words will flow next. Yet everything that is happening seems totally unbelievable. To ease the confusion in my mind with all of the emerging aspects and their changing titles, I create the following chart to give some order.

Chart of Aspects as of June 12, 2012

New Name	Previous Name	Date First Noted	Date Fully Integrated
Tenacity	Rigid Taskmaster	4-7-12	5-8-12
Courage	Stern Enforcer	4-7-12	5-8-12
Flexible	Saboteur	6-4-12	
	Defective	6-12-12	
Beloved	Unlovable	6-12-12	
Precious	Unworthy	6-12-12	

Chapter 2

Focus on the
Divine Within

June 20, 2012

THIS ENTIRE PROCESS IS emotional for me. I realize I must find a location outside of my home to effectively continue. I never know when I might cry or need to make disturbing noises. For today, I continue at home.

With determination to avoid possible health issues, I do all the inner-child work suggested by John Bradshaw. As I move through the exercises, however, I discover I can actually dialogue with the parts of myself I am uncovering through my inner-child work. This adds incredible depth to my process and feels beneficial. With this in mind, I look over my list of flawed core beliefs, which are named Perfectionist, Guilt, and Overwhelmed and Confused. I get a yes that Overwhelmed and Confused is willing to start. (See appendix A for information about getting yes-or-no answers to questions.)

EMILY. I now open a dialogue with Overwhelmed and Confused.

I see an image in my mind of a figure bent over at the waist with arms dangling.

EMILY. Is this you, Overwhelmed and Confused?

OVERWHELMED AND CONFUSED. Yes, it is I.

EMILY. Would you please talk to me about what is going on with you?

OVERWHELMED AND CONFUSED. Well, I am not a good talker.

EMILY. That is all right. Just do your best.

OVERWHELMED AND CONFUSED. But I am so tired. I have the others, you know, the ones you mentioned above, all pressing down on me all the time. How can I ever be anything else? I do not like this. I want to move, dance, and play, but I have to please the others.

EMILY. Why?

OVERWHELMED AND CONFUSED. I don't know. Would you please help me find out? I am not happy. Please help me. I am relieved you finally noticed me. That helps me a lot.

EMILY. Thank you. I hope I can help you. Are you ready to make any changes?

OVERWHELMED AND CONFUSED. Not until the others move first. I am powerless to change until they change.

EMILY. Thank you. This is helpful information. I love you.

OVERWHELMED AND CONFUSED. I love you too. And thank you again for noticing.

I hold a simple candle ceremony to welcome Tenacity and Courage to the team.

July 9, 2012

I continue with my list of flawed core beliefs.

EMILY. I now open a dialogue with the part of me I call Perfectionist. Are you willing to talk to me at this time?

PERFECTIONIST. I am not sure. I am not willing to be transformed like the others. I have been with you for a long time, and I feel I have served you well.

EMILY. Oh, I know you have served me well, and that includes even now. I do not want you to go away. I just need to relax and be more flexible. There is that word again. It is one I do not feel comfortable with, but it is an aspect that needs to be a part of me at this time. Do you agree?

PERFECTIONIST. Yes, I can see where that would be helpful for you. I just don't like change. How do you know being more flexible will not lead us the wrong way?

EMILY. That is interesting. I am not sure there is a right or wrong way.

PERFECTIONIST. I do not like that kind of thinking. That makes me uncomfortable.

EMILY. Thank you for sharing and being so honest.

PERFECTIONIST. I always try to please.

EMILY. Yes, I know you do. It is this always trying to please others that is bothering me. I am determined to free us from that role.

PERFECTIONIST. I don't know what to say. I can't remember when we did not try to please all others around us. What if we made someone else angry? That would be scary. Oh, I just don't know about this flexibility stuff at all.

EMILY. I understand. What if you try to be flexible for, say, one week, and then we will talk some more?

PERFECTIONIST. I know you don't mean that. It is just a ploy to get me to change.

EMILY. Hold on a minute. I just had a thought. I am going to look back to see what other part had to do with flexibility. Oh, I just remembered. It was my saboteur part [see June 4, 2012]. Perfectionist, are you connected with Saboteur?

PERFECTIONIST. I don't think so, as I am the good one, and Saboteur is the bad one.

EMILY. There is that black-and-white thinking again.

PERFECTIONIST. Well, it is true.

EMILY. I feel the need to talk to Saboteur, possibly called Flexible. Please stand by.

PERFECTIONIST. All right.

EMILY. I would now like to talk to Saboteur, please. I thought you had transformed to Flexible.

SABOTEUR. Oh, I am Flexible. Perfectionist just doesn't want to accept me. She is tricky that way, and all those words about good and bad? Rubbish! We are all one—just different aspects.

EMILY. I am at a loss here. Does all this balking have to do with a forgiveness project, as suggested in my astrology reading, which I am currently working through?

SABOTEUR. I am afraid it does, but I can't speak for Perfectionist.

PERFECTIONIST. I am not going to change anyway, but you are free to go ahead and try. I think I have more to do with your accommodator role anyway.

EMILY. Thank you both for sharing. Are you ready to join the team, Flexible?

FLEXIBLE. I don't know anything about being flexible.

EMILY. Me neither! I will ask again at another time.

July 13, 2012

I mention to several friends my need for a private place where I can do my work, and a friend happens to have a garage studio I am free to use. Today I begin in this new private space. Through my inner-child exercises, I identify more flawed core beliefs. One of these beliefs I title Judgment and Critical Eye.

EMILY. Are you willing to dialogue with me at this time, Judgment and Critical Eye? I am a little nervous about this. May I call you Judge's Eye for short?

JUDGE'S EYE. I prefer Judge's Eye if you please, and yes, I will dialogue with you.

EMILY. Thank you for being willing. Would you please tell me about yourself?

JUDGE'S EYE. Well, what do you know? We are finally in a conversation. You've used my skills effectively many times over the years. We are old companions. I help you make sense out of a world that makes no sense. That is still true. I do not see how you would want to make any modifications to my part at all. I'm the one who helps you to be perfect, after all.

EMILY. I do not understand your last statement. Please explain further.

JUDGE'S EYE. Well, I tell you what is proper and what is not, such as another's smoking too near you or driving polluting cars—the list goes on and on. I help you judge honestly.

EMILY. I see. Thank you. I appreciate all you have done for me up until this time, but I feel now that you are too rigid, and this keeps negative energy stuck in my body. This is not good for my cells and my body. I think you agree, as you seem to want to help me.

JUDGE'S EYE. I wish only to help you and to be of service. I see what you mean. Do you have suggestions?

EMILY. I am looking for your beneficial side. I will let words flow, and you stop me when you come to something that appeals. Discernment?

JUDGE'S EYE. I don't really understand that word.

EMILY. Acceptance?

JUDGE'S EYE. That is much better, but what if you don't accept what another is doing?

EMILY. Good question. I am learning to leave that up to God.

JUDGE'S EYE. I thought you were just questioning that the divine was even within you.

EMILY. There must be a way not to take on negative energy when I see people doing things I do not approve of. They are leading their lives, and I am leading mine. We each have our own paths to follow. I cannot change another. I do not have any power over another. All I can do is let them be who they are. Is that it? Let Them Be? Are you willing to be called Let Them Be?

JUDGE'S EYE. Highly unusual name, but I think it suits your purpose, and I agree that your body's cells are most important to both of us. Yes, I agree.

EMILY. Oh, I am so grateful! Thank you so much for this dialogue. Yes, Let Them Be is a beautiful name. I just realized that the name also needs to include me. What do you think about Let It Be?

JUDGE'S EYE. Oh, I like that even better.

EMILY. Thank you. The word *it* includes people, places, and things.

I hope this shift in perspective will help me to be calmer about all of life outside my body as well as inside my body.

EMILY. This feels very wise—like the song that goes, "Speaking words of wisdom, let it be. Let it be." Are you willing to join the team at this time, Let It Be?

LET IT BE. I am most honored to be a part of the team.

I do a simple candle ceremony of welcome. I now have Tenacity, Courage, and Let It Be on my team.

July 25, 2012

I am led to try a dialogue with a part of myself that showed up in a dream of June 8, 2012, in which I met a sick hospital patient. At the end of the dream, I was awake enough to ask who was being represented, and I heard the word *self-esteem*.

EMILY. Are you willing to talk with me, Self-Esteem? Are you still the sick hospital patient?

SELF-ESTEEM. Yes, I am willing but barely, and yes, I am still very sick, but I've felt much better since you did the forgiveness project. That was helpful. I actually think I will be able to fully heal. Please keep talking to me.

EMILY. Do you have a story to tell me?

SELF-ESTEEM. Yes, I have a story. I was almost crushed out of existence during your high school years, but I survived. I would like you to acknowledge me more often. You may wish to include humility if you are concerned you will get too puffed up, but I do not think that is necessary. If you focus on the divine within more and more, your ego will not want to get in the way.

EMILY. This is wise of you. Thank you for sharing. I'm just beginning to trust that the divine is indeed within me.

SELF-ESTEEM. How can you doubt for one minute after the amazing experiences you have been having? This is why I am still not totally well.

EMILY. Do you have any suggestions to help with our healing?

SELF-ESTEEM. Yes, I do.

EMILY. Would you please share them with me?

SELF-ESTEEM. Well, all right since you asked. I would like you to hug me more. Tell me you love me out loud every day, at least until it soaks in, and say out loud that you behold the divine within me. Can you do that?

EMILY. Oh yes. I can do that. I know the out-loud part will be a challenge, but I can do it.

SELF-ESTEEM. Yes, but you asked, and it is important for me.

EMILY. Are you ready to join the team?

SELF-ESTEEM. Yes, but I need to see that you follow through on your words before I will agree. Ask me next week.

EMILY. Thank you. I have you on the calendar. Will you help remind me?

SELF-ESTEEM. No, you have to remember for yourself if it is important—rather, if I am important.

EMILY. That is fair. Thank you. I will have to say it until I believe it.

SELF-ESTEEM. Yes, that is true.

Chart of Aspects as of July 25, 2012

New Name	Previous Name	Date First Noted	Date Fully Integrated
Tenacity	Rigid Taskmaster	4-7-12	5-8-12
Courage	Stern Enforcer	4-7-12	5-8-12
Flexible	Saboteur	6-4-12	
	Defective	6-12-12	
Beloved	Unlovable	6-12-12	
Precious	Unworthy	6-12-12	
	Overwhelmed and Confused	6-20-12	
	Guilt	6-20-12	
	Perfectionist	7-9-12	
Let It Be	Judge's Eye	7-13-12	7-13-12
Self-Esteem	Sick Hospital Patient	7-25-12	

BREATHE

Chapter 3

I Am Worthy of God's Love

July 30, 2012

RECENTLY, AN ENERGY DOWSER and healer friend of mine, Michael Hoefler, told me I have two parts who are related to my inability to allow God's love. I decide to investigate this comment. I have a feeling these parts may be Unlovable and Unworthy, and I was given new names for them on June 12, 2012. Unlovable is now Beloved, and Unworthy is now Precious. With pen and notebook ready, I begin a dialogue.

EMILY. I now open a dialogue with Beloved. I have done the forgiveness process. It was extremely powerful. Do you think I am on the first step of allowing God's love and, therefore, you to merge with me?

BELOVED. Oh! You are far past the first step. You are about halfway to full integration. Give yourself time. You are doing well. The assignment given to you by Self-Esteem to sit daily and open yourself to God's love will complete the integration.

EMILY. I am thrilled to learn this. I still feel wobbly.

BELOVED. That is only because this is new for you. And I see you are pondering whether or not to go to a workshop. There is no need for you to get sidetracked with third-eye opening at this time. This will come more easily later, when you have integrated your fragmented parts. There is no rush but a mild urgency.

EMILY. Thank you. Do you think it is possible for me to open a dialogue with Precious, previously called Unworthy?

BELOVED. Please try. Just relax and allow. We love you.

EMILY. I am confused. I thought you were a fragmented part, and now you use the pronoun *we*.

BELOVED. Only because we are a small group, but we act as one. We will integrate fully with you when you are open and ready to fully allow God's magnificent love. Relax, and enjoy!

EMILY. I am now ready to open a dialogue with Precious, formerly called Unworthy. Are you willing to dialogue with me, Precious?

PRECIOUS. I have been waiting for this moment for a long time. I am thrilled to dialogue with you, dear Emily. Again, I have always been close to you, and I have helped you as much as you would allow. Now it is time to fully embrace me and allow me to totally love you. I have always loved you, and I always will. You are worthy. You did not need to do the forgiveness work before I would love you, because I have never stopped loving you, but you did need to do it for yourself so that you would feel worthy to accept my love.

EMILY. I am so grateful. Yes, I am beginning to feel worthy of your love. Do you have any assignments for me to help with this process?

PRECIOUS. Every day until you believe it, say, "I am worthy of God's love. I am precious in God's sight." It might take a while, but know that you are worthy, so it will happen. Relax, and enjoy!

EMILY. Are you and Beloved the two fractured parts related to my allowing God's love, as mentioned by Michael Hoefler, my energy dowser and healer friend?

PRECIOUS. Yes, we are. We go hand in hand, so to speak, which is why you keep hearing *I* and *we* almost interchangeably.

EMILY. Thank you for the clarification. This is important to me. I want to be totally clear. What a marvelous assignment! I rest now in God's loving arms. Thank you, Precious, and thank you, Beloved. I love you both very much!

August 2, 2012

I had a dream on July 23, 2012, that repeated again last night, titled Safety Team on Mountain. In it, I am walking through a jungle on the way up a mountain. At first, I am following a wide bark-chip path, but it soon becomes a narrow, bare dirt trail, and the jungle seems to be closing in. I see a huge white machine coming my way on the path, and men are working all over the area. They wear hard hats and overalls. The machine has a rotating blade like an egg beater that obliterates my path.

At the end of the dream, I am aware enough to ask who the workmen are and why they are stopping me. I hear that they are my safety team and my security force. They say they are not happy with all this talk about communicating with the unseen world. They say I am shaking up their world, and they are concerned for my good.

August 3, 2012

I get a yes that I am to dialogue with the above dream aspects.

EMILY. I now open a dialogue with Safety Team and Security Force. Are you ready to dialogue with me?

SAFETY TEAM AND SECURITY FORCE. Yes. We want to talk to you urgently. We see you getting almost reckless.

EMILY. All right, but first, do you need both terms in your long title?

SAFETY TEAM AND SECURITY FORCE. Yes, you need both aspects of us, the safety and the security, the team and the force.

EMILY. Thank you. Why did you stop me from going up the mountain?

SAFETY TEAM AND SECURITY FORCE. We already told you.

EMILY. I remember, but I did not like your answer. Are you fragmented parts of me who split off during my childhood?

I have come to think of my aspects as fragmented parts that I must integrate with to become a more whole person.

SAFETY TEAM AND SECURITY FORCE. Yes, we are, but most of us stayed with you. We watch over you and keep you from doing silly and dangerous things.

EMILY. Thank you, and I appreciate your help very much. However, I feel strongly that the dialogues I am having with my other aspects are helpful to me. I do not understand your reluctance for me to talk to the unseen world. Please explain.

SAFETY TEAM AND SECURITY FORCE. Oh, talking to your aspects would be fine, but we do not like the idea of you opening yourself to the entire unseen world without us to protect you. We feel strongly about this.

EMILY. This is interesting. Are you saying I need to call in a spiritual support team, such as Jesus, the archangels, and my higher self, whenever I do this writing?

SAFETY TEAM AND SECURITY FORCE. Oh, most assuredly, yes! Look, you did not even do this a few minutes ago when we began. You also need divine light around your energy field when you do any dialoguing with the unseen world. It only takes a minute, and we would feel much better and safer. You are naive and do not know that all energies are for your benefit. You are connecting with those you already know at this time, but we want you to make a conscious habit of calling in all those mentioned. It is all right to add other spiritual helpers when you sense they might be needed.

EMILY. Thank you very much. Do you have any comments about my recent statement that I am feeling less cautious these days?

SAFETY TEAM AND SECURITY FORCE. We do not mind, as it shows you are getting stronger. We only have concern over your lack of spiritual help. The work you are doing is not to be taken lightly. We will always be here for you.

EMILY. Thank you. Are you ready to integrate with me fully at this time?

I quickly call in all of the above mentioned spiritual helpers.

SAFETY TEAM AND SECURITY FORCE. We are ready to integrate fully at this time.

EMILY. Are you ready to be a part of the team?

SAFETY TEAM AND SECURITY FORCE. We are ready to join. We are a spiritual protection system. We work with the unseen world, and we are honored to join the team.

EMILY. Welcome to the team! I love you.

SAFETY TEAM AND SECURITY FORCE. We love you as well and always have.

I have the thought that I am enjoying contacting my fractured aspects, and I do not want these intriguing dialogues to end. I immediately hear, "Oh, this is just the beginning of our dialogues. Not to worry." I continue with my list of flawed core beliefs.

EMILY. I now open a dialogue with Guilt. Do you have comments for me?

GUILT. Yes, and there is a healthy aspect to my energy called conscience. Even though you have released the majority of my negative energy during your forgiveness processes, there is this positive side I want you to keep and always be aware of. Just know I am here for you, and I will get your attention if needed. I am proud of you and pleased with all the inner work you are doing. Remember to have some fun too.

I feel a slight twinge at this comment, as play is not easy for me, and I hear the following:

GUILT. This is what I mean by getting your attention. You will feel a small twinge inside, and that is me reminding you.

EMILY. Do you mean you are now fully integrated?

GUILT. No, you need to ask me first.

EMILY. Does this mean I do not need to find a new name for you, or is that Conscience?

CONSCIENCE. Yes, that is my healthy name.

EMILY. Would you please be a part of the team?

CONSCIENCE. I would be honored to be a part of the team.

EMILY. Thank you so much. I love you.

CONSCIENCE. I love you also.

Chart of Aspects as of August 3, 2012

New Name	Previous Name	Date First Noted	Date Fully Integrated
Tenacity	Rigid Taskmaster	4-7-12	5-8-12
Courage	Stern Enforcer	4-7-12	5-8-12
Flexible	Saboteur	6-4-12	
	Defective	6-12-12	
Beloved	Unlovable	6-12-12	
Precious	Unworthy	6-12-12	
	Overwhelmed and Confused	6-20-12	
Conscience	Guilt	6-20-12	8-3-12
	Perfectionist	7-9-12	
Let It Be	Judge's Eye	7-13-12	7-13-12
Self-Esteem	Sick Hospital Patient	7-25-12	
Safety Team and Security Force	Safety Team and Security Force	8-3-12	8-3-12

Chapter 4

An Intuitive Hunch

August 6, 2012

At the garage studio, I call in my spiritual support team. Through my inner-child work, I have developed a list of my dysfunctional family roles. I am curious to learn if they are also aspects of myself, as my flawed core beliefs are. I attempt a dialogue.

EMILY. Are you ready and willing to dialogue with me, Super-Responsible One?

SUPER-RESPONSIBLE ONE. I am shy about dialoguing because there is a person working in the yard outside the window.

EMILY. I know, but I promise I will be quiet and discreet. I don't think she will know we are in this unused studio space. Will that help?

SUPER-RESPONSIBLE ONE. Yes, I am willing to proceed.

EMILY. Do you have anything you would like to say to me at this time?

SUPER-RESPONSIBLE ONE. Well, I am not sure. I don't know why I am being called on the carpet, so to speak.

EMILY. I am attempting to get to know the various aspects of myself and to integrate with them where appropriate.

SUPER-RESPONSIBLE ONE. Well, I am above most of the others. They take orders from me. I am the boss, and I decide what is appropriate for the others to do, so it is time we had a chat.

EMILY. That sounds great. What do you have to say to me about yourself?

SUPER-RESPONSIBLE ONE. Are you sure you want me to talk?

EMILY. Yes, I'm sure. Please continue.

SUPER-RESPONSIBLE ONE. I think I just told you all I want to say at this time. I am not about to be talked into changing, as I am too important.

EMILY. Yes, you are important to me. I am concerned, though, about the cells of our body and what happens to them when I feel I must take on responsibility for the actions, words, and feelings of others. I have been doing that for a long time, and I do not think it serves either of us at this time. Do you have comments?

SUPER-RESPONSIBLE ONE. Not really. By being responsible, as you call it, for the others, especially for the feelings of others, you were able to navigate through an extremely demanding childhood. I think you can drop the "super-responsible" part, though, as you are not and never were able to make others feel differently. You just thought you could. I never said you could. I just helped give you those messages.

EMILY. Oh! Are you really my sensitivity or my intuition?

SUPER-RESPONSIBLE ONE. Yes, I am your intuition with my own version. You have not been good about listening to me until, well, the last few months. I am surprised.

EMILY. What do you mean by your own version?

SUPER-RESPONSIBLE ONE. I am still above the others. You keep skipping that part.

EMILY. I would love to be closer to my intuition. I do not understand what you mean by being above the others. Please explain.

SUPER-RESPONSIBLE ONE. I am more closely connected to our higher self.

EMILY. Thank you. May I start calling you Intuition instead of Super-Responsible One?

SUPER-RESPONSIBLE ONE. Yes, that would be fine.

EMILY. Thank you. I think you are already a part of my team, but I would like to formally acknowledge you. Is that all right?

INTUITION. Oh, I think that is most appropriate, and I think it is about time I get some acknowledgment. After all, I have been serving you since birth—well, actually, before.

EMILY. I am thrilled to acknowledge you. Welcome to the team, Intuition. You are now here with Tenacity, Courage, Conscience, Let It Be, and Safety Team and Security Force.

INTUITION. I am honored, and I accept this acknowledgment.

EMILY. I would like to get to know you better, but I feel the need to learn about and integrate with other aspects. Are you fully integrated with me at this time? May we close for now?

INTUITION. Yes, and yes. I have much to teach you when you are ready to listen. Please do not forget about me.

EMILY. I look forward to learning more. Do you agree that I need to integrate with the others now?

INTUITION. That question is a good example of what I will be teaching, which is to never second-guess an intuitive hunch. Once given, it is not given again in the same way.

EMILY. Oh! Thank you so much.

I do a celebration to welcome Intuition. The person gardening outside is gone, so I sing and dance around the studio.

During an inner-child exercise involving my four-and-a-half-year-old self, I identify a character trait of sadness. Since I have been able to dialogue with my flawed core beliefs and dysfunctional family roles, I decide to try a dialogue with this character trait.

EMILY. Sadness, are you ready and willing to talk to me?

SADNESS. I don't know. I am quite tired. Can we rest first?

EMILY. Yes. I will relax and close my eyes for a bit.

I lean back on the couch and rest my eyes for a minute, when I start to hear some words.

EMILY. Are you ready to continue?

SADNESS. Yes. I am from the time when you shut down your joy. You stopped feeling your own inner joy when you were four and a half years old. I started to come back when your two daughters were young, but that did not continue. I just want to be noticed, like you just did with Intuition. That is all I ask.

EMILY. My heart goes out to you, dear one, but I am not crying. Have I already cried all the tears?

SADNESS. This is odd, but I think you are right. What I really want to do is morph into Joy. Can we do that?

EMILY. We can do anything that feels appropriate, and this feels great to me. Is it this easy? We just decide to evolve you into Joy, and it is done?

SADNESS. It seems so. Yes, I want you to call me Joy from now on!

EMILY. Yippee! Are you ready to join the team?

I can't believe this is happening, but I continue anyway.

JOY. Yes, I am ready to join the team. You really do need me. You are trying, but you are so serious! Let's get some life into this dialoguing! That's it—some John Philip Sousa music and dancing! And yes, I want to go to the meditation group tonight, even if all the vacuuming is not done. Okay? Can you go along with me this time if I ask nicely? Please?

EMILY. All right. Here we go. I am excited to have you on the team, but you know I am not used to this.

I do my best to vocalize some marching tunes as I dance about the studio space.

JOY. Oh yes, I know, but you will get used to me and will come to really love having me around. Let's celebrate!

EMILY. Yes, does this mean you are ready to fully integrate with me now?

JOY. Of course I am! And please stop being so formal, and do not list all the other members. Let's play!

August 7, 2012

I meet with Georgie and share my inner-child work. This day, Georgie and I have a conversation about God's love. I explain that I know there is a God, but it is difficult for me to feel that God notices me, let alone that God loves me. I ask, "How can I open myself to receive more of God's love?" Georgie replies, "God is always here, and it is up to us to allow God's love." I ponder this comment.

August 11, 2012

I call in my spiritual support team and continue to explore these amazing aspects of myself.

EMILY. I am ready to open a dialogue with Defective. Are you willing to dialogue with me today?

DEFECTIVE. Yes, I think so.

EMILY. I'll take that as a yes. Do you have anything to say to me at this time?

DEFECTIVE. I just do what I know to be true. As I look over the evidence of our life, I see that I still belong. I am an aspect you adapted in your early childhood to explain why you were so miserable. I do not know what to say. Until you are ready to let go of me, I will be with you. I do have a positive side, and that is to prevent arrogance. Arrogance is not helpful. It blocks truth. You can be inclined in that direction easily, as you want to feel good about yourself. You have not felt good about yourself for many years.

EMILY. Thank you so much. I want to feel good about myself. Is there a way to balance these two somewhat opposite traits of arrogance and defectiveness with a more positive wholeness? The word *balance* keeps coming to my mind. Do you think *balance* is a more positive word for your helping me not to be too arrogant?

DEFECTIVE. Yes, I really like that word! I would like to be called Balanced. That feels calm, even, and fair. Yes, I really like that.

EMILY. Thank you. Would you like to join the team?

BALANCED. Yes, I would, but you need to do something about Inadequate first.

EMILY. Thank you. I now open a dialogue with Inadequate. Are you willing to dialogue with me today?

INADEQUATE. Yes, I am more fundamental than Balanced, formerly Defective. You also took on aspects of me in your early childhood.

EMILY. Do you have more comments for me?

INADEQUATE. You will have to release me and then do forgiveness work. I am also linked to Perfectionist and Pity.

EMILY. All right. I declare, "I now release the belief that I am inadequate."

The thought comes to me that I need to do EFT tapping as I let go of this belief. Somehow, I know that the release of this belief will be healing not only for myself but also for all members of my family and my family lineage. As I begin the forgiveness part, however, I find much anger I need to release first. I continue EFT tapping as I release anger. Finally, I feel better and know the anger has been released.

I move to forgiveness and continue until I feel complete.

Then I get the message inside my head that when I fully integrate with Beloved and Precious, this belief in being inadequate will be 100 percent gone.

EMILY. Is there a positive side that I can call you, Inadequate?

INADEQUATE. Yes, you can call me Strength.

EMILY. Amazing! I was just wondering if that trait would ever come up.

This is always a surprise. I never know ahead of time what my aspects will morph into.

EMILY. Thank you, Strength. Please join the team! Balanced, are you now ready and willing to join the team?

BALANCED. I am.

EMILY. I lovingly welcome Strength and Balanced. I am pleased to have you with me.

I did some deep inner work last night to help release my people-pleaser role.

EMILY. I now open a dialogue with Perfectionist. Are you willing to dialogue with me at this time?

PERFECTIONIST. Yes, I am willing to talk at this time. You did some commendable work last night. I am not convinced it will last, but it was something. Yes, it was.

EMILY. Thank you for the acknowledgment. My two-and-a-half-year-old Little Emily and I feel much better today. Do you have any more to say to me now?

PERFECTIONIST. I'm quite tired. I don't know if this is a good time for me to go on.

EMILY. All right. How about if we wait for a day or two?

PERFECTIONIST. That would be much better.

EMILY. I was hoping that after all the work I did last night, I could buzz right through with our talk today.

PERFECTIONIST. There will be no buzzing with me. I do not see much need for me to be involved in a dialogue.

EMILY. The constant need for perfection and to have everything under control takes all the fun, joy, and spontaneity out of my life.

PERFECTIONIST. Yes, I see that, but I don't see us ever being unprepared.

EMILY. I don't mean being unprepared. I mean having to be right and know all the answers and not allowing myself to ever relax or not be right. You know, they say there is no real right or wrong anyway. Life is to be experienced, not orchestrated. I still want to be able to interact with people and teach, but I also want to be able to laugh, let down my guard, and have some fun in the process. I want to be able to relax without needing to have all the answers or striving for perfection at all times.

PERFECTIONIST. I suppose you have a point there. Well, I will consider this for a few days. I always keep you organized, you know. Without me, things you do would be a mess.

EMILY. I like the word *organized*. What do you think about that for a title?

PERFECTIONIST. I like it a lot!

EMILY. May I call you Organized instead of Perfectionist?

PERFECTIONIST. Well, I think Organized is delightful. I do not make rash decisions, though. Get back to me in a day or two, if you please.

EMILY. I will be most happy to do that. See you later, alligator!

PERFECTIONIST. Oh, don't do that. It is so silly. I don't know what to do with you if you get silly. You might be irresponsible.

EMILY. I know you are concerned. I will think about being playful and being responsible at the same time. I think it is possible!

PERFECTIONIST. Oh, I just don't know. I just care so deeply for you and all you do.

EMILY. I am touched by your caring. I thank you for all you have done for me and for all you do for me. *Caring* is a nice word also.

PERFECTIONIST. That is part of Beloved.

Chart of Aspects as of August 11, 2012

New Name	Previous Name	Date First Noted	Date Fully Integrated
Tenacity	Rigid Taskmaster	4-7-12	5-8-12
Courage	Stern Enforcer	4-7-12	5-8-12
Flexible	Saboteur	6-4-12	
Balanced	Defective	6-12-12	8-11-12
Beloved	Unlovable	6-12-12	
Precious	Unworthy	6-12-12	
	Overwhelmed and Confused	6-20-12	
Conscience	Guilt	6-20-12	8-3-12
Organized	Perfectionist	7-9-12	
Let It Be	Judge's Eye	7-13-12	7-13-12
Self-Esteem	Sick Hospital Patient	7-25-12	
Safety Team and Security Force	Safety Team and Security Force	8-3-12	8-3-12
Intuition	Super-Responsible One	8-6-12	8-6-12
Joy	Sadness	8-6-12	8-6-12
Strength	Inadequate	8-11-12	8-11-12

Chapter 5

Free at Last

August 13, 2012

I CALL IN MY support team. Today I look over my list of aspects and get a yes that Perfectionist would like to dialogue.

EMILY. I now open a dialogue with Perfectionist. Are you willing to dialogue with me?

PERFECTIONIST. I most certainly am.

EMILY. Thank you. The last time we talked two days ago, the word *organized* came to me, and you wished to have some time to consider this title. Do you have comments now?

PERFECTIONIST. I am most honored with this new title. It is not a change, for it is who I am, but I do like the sound and feeling of the noble title of Organized. You may refer to me as Organized from now on. Thank you.

EMILY. Oh, thank you so much. You have been helping me get organized for the big events I have coming up, have you not?

ORGANIZED. I certainly have been helping—like the way that paper from your friend just showed up.

EMILY. I am thrilled and grateful. Are you ready to fully integrate with the team at this time?

ORGANIZED. Absolutely. And I might suggest you bring a dictionary when you come to the studio for your dialogues.

EMILY. Good idea. That will help me feel better about spelling. Also, I am noticing that I feel calm and relaxed with your energy this afternoon. In the past, I felt anxious when we dialogued. Welcome to the team, Organized!

I get a yes that Overwhelmed and Confused would like to dialogue.

EMILY. I open a dialogue with Overwhelmed and Confused. Are you willing to talk with me?

OVERWHELMED AND CONFUSED. Yes, I am.

EMILY. Thank you. First, I need a clarification. On June 13, 2012, I had a dream about a woman who needed a bath and said she couldn't see well. I hugged her, and she began to cry. Then, on June 24, 2012, I had a dream about a woman who was hit in the mouth with a baseball. She could not speak well, but she was intelligent. Are these totally different aspects I need to address separately, or are they all the same part with different faces? Overwhelmed and Confused, can you answer these questions?

OVERWHELMED AND CONFUSED. Actually, I can. Yes, we are all faces of the same part. I am that part.

EMILY. In our first dialogue, you told me you were not a good talker. Thank you for your tenacity and courage to keep trying to get my attention through dreams. I appreciate this. I remember you being all bent over and pushed down with the weight of the others on top of you [see chapter 2]. The others, Perfectionist and Guilt, now have new titles. They are now Organized and Conscience. I see you are still quite sad, overwhelmed, and confused.

OVERWHELMED AND CONFUSED. I am still quite sad, but I think I am much less overwhelmed and confused.

EMILY. Do you need some holding and support before we continue?

OVERWHELMED AND CONFUSED. Yes, I would like that. I have been sad for a long time. I do not know how to feel happy.

EMILY. I see you are not bent over today like the last time.

OVERWHELMED AND CONFUSED. That is right. I am standing on my own two feet on the earth.

EMILY. I give you huge hugs. Let's dance around the room. All right?

OVERWHELMED AND CONFUSED. Yes, I would like that. I am such a sad mess, though.

EMILY. No one will see us. We are safe here. Let's try, okay?

OVERWHELMED AND CONFUSED. All right.

I sing as I dance around the studio while holding my unseen part.

EMILY. Come with me. Come with me. Come with me, Overwhelmed and Confused!

I pause to dry my tears.

EMILY. I sense you are overwhelmed and not ready to talk about other titles today, but these words came to me: *playful, play,* and *imagination.* Are you able to choose one today?

OVERWHELMED AND CONFUSED. No, I am too overwhelmed and confused.

EMILY. I would like to suggest you just sit with these feelings until we meet again. You are much stronger now than you think. Another title of Clarity just came to me. What do you think of that?

OVERWHELMED AND CONFUSED. Oh, I could never be Clarity. That is a grand title.

EMILY. Why not? You get to choose. Why not choose the best one?

OVERWHELMED AND CONFUSED. What if I cannot possibly ever be clear?

EMILY. Who says you cannot be clear?

OVERWHELMED AND CONFUSED. Well, I just know I can't be clear. Look at my past.

EMILY. I see you as one who has not been allowed to dance in joy and feel good about herself. I see you as being calm, serene, and poised and then springing into joyous laughter and dancing around the room, sure of herself. I see you as one who acts on divine guidance with clarity and grace. There is another wonderful word: *grace.* Well, I leave you for today. There is no rush, but know that you have done a huge amount of shifting this day. I love you and look forward to the next time we meet.

OVERWHELMED AND CONFUSED. I love you too. I am grateful you noticed me.

EMILY. Grateful is a good title as well. It will come to you. Do not try to decide now. You will be led to the right and perfect title in the right time.

August 27, 2012

I call in my support team. I continue my dialogues to uncover more information about my flawed core beliefs. I get a yes to dialogue with Pity.

EMILY. I now open a dialogue with Pity. I know you well, as you have been with me for many years, from about the time I was four and a half years old. I do not feel you as much these days, but you were significant in my childhood.

As a little girl, when life got too much for me, I would go off by myself; sink into deep self-pity; and have a good, long cry. Then I would feel better and be able to carry on. These were my own invented counseling sessions.

EMILY. Do you have any comments for me?

PITY. Yes, I would like to dialogue with you very much. You know how much I helped you survive your school-age years. I was always there to help you shed those tears and release pent-up emotions. I do not think you would have survived without me.

EMILY. Yes, you are correct. I am grateful for your help. I had no other tools, and no one else was able to help me. Thank you very much. I would now like to see if you have a positive side. Do you?

PITY. I don't know what you mean.

EMILY. You allowed me a way to release emotions, but now I am learning to let emotions flow through my body without needing to go into self-pity first. That kind of self-pity is not good for our cells. Do you agree?

PITY. Yes, I do agree, and I am glad you do not need to utilize my services for that purpose, but what about your pity of others? Or when you sense others are looking at you with pity?

EMILY. I am learning that one never knows what a soul is trying to accomplish in this life. That has allowed me to accept others much more for who they are. This process of acceptance, both for myself and others, is new for me. What do you think about being called Acceptance? That covers a wide range of emotions, but it feels good to me.

PITY. This will not be easy.

EMILY. I am just realizing that. I don't know if I am ready. Will you help me? I think this means accepting my life and everything about it just as it is and saying it is all right. This will take some transformation. Do you have comments?

PITY. This is a big step to take. Rest for a few minutes, and let it soak in.

EMILY. I will do that. In fact, I will wait and talk to Georgie tomorrow about all of this. I feel tired now. Is that all right with you?

PITY. Certainly. Self-care is a part of your transformation, but what you did as a young girl and for much of your life was self-care too. Do not judge yourself so harshly.

EMILY. There is a part of me that does not want to accept my life. I have been so focused on changing my unhappy life, and I do feel much better now than before. I am confused about this acceptance part.

PITY. Ask Georgie.

EMILY. Yes, I will. Thank you, Pity, for your help today.

I know I need to release self-pity, so I invent my own release process. I visualize self-pity leaving me and going back to the universe. I do EFT tapping. Suddenly, I realize there is much anger underneath the self-pity. I make my anger sounds and release anger for the years of self-pity. At last, I feel calm and strong.

I continue my inner exploration with a dysfunctional family role I call Shy One.

EMILY. I now open a dialogue with Shy One. First, let me say thank you for agreeing to talk to me. I know this is taking a lot of courage for you. A few months ago, Georgie gave me the idea that you might be a role I learned to play and that maybe it is not who I really am. Are you ready and willing to dialogue with me?

SHY ONE. Oh yes, I am ready. I am ready to kick out the sides of this box I have been in for so many years. It is time. Yes, it is about time!

EMILY. You do not seem very shy to me. Is it true that being shy was a role I learned early on in order to stay as invisible as possible, which meant I was as safe as possible?

SHY ONE. You are absolutely right on. You did not feel safe in your body the whole time you grew up. In fact, you are just now beginning to feel safe in your body. I am glad! Our bodies are to be enjoyed, and you have to make up for a lot of lost time. That is a joke, of course. There is really all the time in the universe, as there is really no time. I love puzzles and grand thinking.

EMILY. I want to get to know you more. What else can you tell me about yourself? And what new title would you like to be called? The word *playful* keeps coming to mind. How do you feel about that?

SHY ONE. That is smashing! Yes, I love being playful. Forget being shy. That was a cover-up, and it worked for all these years, but it is time to let it go, and I want to have a ceremony!

EMILY. That's great! Sounds like you are ready to be called Playful and to join the team. Yes?

PLAYFUL. Yippee! You bet I'm ready! I'm glad to be free. Yes, free at last! I thought you would never get around to calling on me. The old role was really safe and stuck in place. Other things needed to shift before the shyness could be released.

EMILY. You are correct. Welcome, Playful!

August 30, 2012

I have a session with Georgie, and we discuss acceptance. Georgie calmly says, "Suppose that accepting yourself exactly as you are is synonymous with being peaceful, calm, and happy." I am stunned. Could this be true? She continues. "This doesn't mean you will stop evolving or listening to your intuition. When you accept who you are, expressing your own uniqueness in the world is God expressing through you as you. Once you accept this, you will trust that this is how you are meant to act in every given moment."

Georgie then says I am forming new neuropathways, so I need a new affirmation, such as "I accept myself the way I am and still I can evolve and grow." She says that when I accept myself, I will know I am beloved and precious.

September 4, 2012

I have a dream in which I see a wire wrapped around a nail. A guru-type person says, "You just have to undo what you have done." An insight comes to me during the dream, and I know this means to undo the negative patterns and behaviors I have established in my life. In the dream, I am not afraid, and I know I am undoing these patterns. As the dream closes, the word *acceptance* comes to me.

September 5, 2012

I call in my support team and practice my new affirmation: "I totally accept myself just the way I am and still I can evolve and grow and then accept again." With curiosity and anticipation, I begin dialogues with the team. I get a yes to open a dialogue with Pity.

EMILY. The last time we spoke, I was not ready to change your title to Acceptance because of the huge change that would involve. Since then, I have been working with the idea of acceptance. Do you have any comments for me?

PITY. I think you are ready to integrate Acceptance as my new title. It is an honor for me, and I gratefully accept. I know both of us are still growing into this new role, but I am confident and delighted that it will unfold in divine order.

EMILY. Thank you so much. Welcome to the team, Acceptance.

ACCEPTANCE. I am honored to be on the team.

I feel acceptance of my life washing down over my shoulders, and I know it is all just right.

EMILY. I am now ready to open a dialogue with Overwhelmed and Confused. Are you ready and willing to dialogue with me?

OVERWHELMED AND CONFUSED. I know I said yes earlier, but now I feel overwhelmed and confused about choosing a new title. You decide for me.

EMILY. Let me list some of the previous words that came to me. They were *support, happy, imagination, clarity, grace,* and *grateful.* What do you think about the name Clarity?

OVERWHELMED AND CONFUSED. Oh, it will be a stretch for me.

EMILY. I know, but last time, you said it was a grand title.

OVERWHELMED AND CONFUSED. Yes, I did, but I went on to say I did not see how I could ever be called Clarity if I am not clear.

EMILY. Yes, I know you said that too, but now I know we are not in this alone. I am just learning that we have an amazing support team, including our own higher self. In fact, I just asked our higher self to join with us today. I am learning that life is a team effort. We are not meant to go it alone. I just had a vision of you dipping your toe into some water. Now I see that you have your whole foot in the water. Now both feet. Now you are standing in the water with a white gown pulled up above your knees. You are in a river. This is like a baptism of sorts.

OVERWHELMED AND CONFUSED. That is just the way I feel.

EMILY. Now I see you in the water, floating on your back with the white gown still on, soaking wet. I think this means you are ready and willing to join the team as Clarity. What do you say?

OVERWHELMED AND CONFUSED. Oh, I don't know what to say, but if you still want me, I will join. I'm feeling scared, though. This is such a huge responsibility. Can't someone else do this part?

EMILY. I don't think so. Remember all I just said and our new affirmation. Life is a learning process. We grow and evolve when the time is right.

I rest for a few minutes to let this soak in.

EMILY. I don't want to push you if you are not ready. But I see you splashing around and playing in the water.

OVERWHELMED AND CONFUSED. I just feel too inadequate to be called Clarity. You know I have trouble talking.

EMILY. I do not think Clarity needs to talk. Clarity just needs to be clear.

OVERWHELMED AND CONFUSED. Well, in that case, I accept.

EMILY. Great! Welcome to the team, Clarity.

Chart of Aspects as of September 5, 2012

New Name	Previous Name	Date First Noted	Date Fully Integrated
Tenacity	Rigid Taskmaster	4-7-12	5-8-12
Courage	Stern Enforcer	4-7-12	5-8-12
Flexible	Saboteur	6-4-12	
Balanced	Defective	6-12-12	8-11-12
Beloved	Unlovable	6-12-12	
Precious	Unworthy	6-12-12	
Clarity	Overwhelmed and Confused	6-20-12	9-5-12
Conscience	Guilt	6-20-12	8-3-12
Organized	Perfectionist	7-9-12	8-13-12
Let It Be	Judge's Eye	7-13-12	7-13-12
Self-Esteem	Sick Hospital Patient	7-25-12	
Safety Team and Security Force	Safety Team and Security Force	8-3-12	8-3-12
Intuition	Super-Responsible One	8-6-12	8-6-12
Joy	Sadness	8-6-12	8-6-12
Strength	Inadequate	8-11-12	8-11-12
Acceptance	Pity	8-27-12	9-5-12
Playful	Shy One	8-27-12	8-27-12

DANCE

Chapter 6

Life Transformation

September 6, 2012

I CONTINUE TO DO all the inner-child exercises from Bradshaw's book *Homecoming*. Today, as I meet with Georgie, we both realize that something amazing is happening. As I do my inner-child work with each age group, I identify parts or aspects of myself. Each aspect seems to be birthed by the experience of the child at that age. For example, Georgie says I "get into the skin" of my two-and-a-half-year-old self, identify aspects I find there, and dialogue with them.

In my dialogue process, I seem to merge with a higher energy field and am easily able to provide the nurturing and love needed by my aspects. My responses come effortlessly in the most loving, competent ways. As a result, my aspects are transforming, and my inner child is being healed. Georgie says this level of inner-child work is deeper than any she has ever seen before.

Additionally, I recently shared some of my aspect dialogues with Mary Jo Wevers, a Jungian karmic astrologer. She described my process as "seeking to reclaim parts of myself that fractured off during traumatic childhood experiences." She suggested I "identify and integrate these parts to feel whole again."

Fascinated by where this is leading me, I take myself on a personal retreat to Breitenbush, a rustic Oregon spa with outdoor hot tubs. I find I need extended periods of alone time to fully explore what is happening in my life.

September 10, 2012

Alone in the beautiful Oregon woods at Breitenbush, I connect with my support team and look over my list of identified aspects. The first to step forward today is Fear, and I am terrified.

I recently told a friend I was doing inner-child work. She immediately said I would need the following tools, which she gave me: large pieces of paper, colored pencils, and a box of soft pastels.

I pull out a piece of paper and the colored pencils.

Using the pencils, I draw an image of Fear. Dark, scary colors come onto the paper. At the end, I pause and breathe until I am ready to continue. Still afraid but curious about what will happen next, I proceed.

This process has moved far beyond my need to avoid possible health issues. I now feel I am engaged in a life-transforming experience.

EMILY. I am now willing to open a dialogue with Fear. Are you willing to dialogue with me?

FEAR. Of course I will talk to you. Why do you think I would be any different from the other aspects? Yes, I am much fractured, and I come in many forms. Fear is a good thing when one is in the middle of the road and a truck is coming toward you. It moves you out of the way. This is about the only time fear is helpful. Now let's talk about all the times you sit in fear that is not helpful and blocks you from taking action.

EMILY. I am tired and need to take a short nap.

FEAR. All right, you can lie down for a short nap, but you have been putting me off all morning, and I am one reason you are doing this retreat in the first place.

EMILY. I know. I won't be long.

I lie down for a minute, and suddenly, I get an image in my mind of prebirth Emily taking fear into her wee body from adults around her. Then I hear, "Fear means disconnection from Source." I sit up, suddenly wide awake and ready to continue.

FEAR. Most of the time when you feel fear, it is because you have disconnected from your God Source. It is a good thing you can feel fear and know what it means. Sometimes it means you need to take action, which is why you have muscles and are able to move. This is a gift from God. All the other times, feeling fear indicates you are disconnected from who you really are, which is connected to your God Source.

EMILY. Time to lie down again.

I rest for a few minutes, and the words *reliable* and *helpful* come to mind. They represent one side of fear. Then the words *connected to God* come to mind. They represent another side. I do not see how fear can morph into connection to God, but I decide to let that be for now.

FEAR. I do not see why you don't see the connection. I just told you about it. When you lie down, you stop being fearful of talking to Fear, and I can slip in and give some insight. It is not a bad way to communicate. In fact, it works quite well. I use it as often as I can—rather, as often as the person will allow.

EMILY. This is all strange. You do seem to know me well and almost sound like a helpful parental figure.

FEAR. Well now, I rather like that image. It suits me much better than the first picture you drew of me. Yes, I like that a lot. Let these radical new ideas soak in for a while, and yes, they are radical—not only for you but also for many others.

EMILY. Thank you. I will do just that.

I rest for a few more minutes.

EMILY. So when I feel fear, it means one of two things: either I move my muscles, or I connect with Source.

FEAR. Exactly. I am necessary for you until you are in a state of total connection to God, and then you will know I am no longer needed.

EMILY. This is amazing. Is this real?

FEAR. It most certainly is real. Jesus was able to live without fear. Constant connection with God equals peace that passes all understanding.

EMILY. Thank you. Now I would like two new titles for you.

I rest a little to see what words come to me. I hear *connected, helpful, takes action, connect to Source,* and *peace.*

EMILY. I just had a thought that has been puzzling me. What is happening when I plan for the future in my mind and fearful thoughts come up? Then I plan again for the future so I will not have the fears, but different fearful thoughts come into my mind. It is an endless cycle.

FEAR. You are practicing creating, but you don't know how, so you are using your mental energy unproductively.

EMILY. Is fear of future events yet another aspect?

FEAR. You can make it one if you like, but it all comes down to disconnection from Source.

EMILY. What about fear regarding the future for my family and loved ones?

FEAR. Same thing. You are disconnected from who you are, and that equals who they are as well.

EMILY. Do you mean we are all connected to Source in our own way?

FEAR. Exactly. You can only see others connected to Source. You cannot do the connection for them. Your visualization will help them, however, and your own connection will be deepened and strengthened.

EMILY. Do you mean that when people in my family leave on a trip, for example, I can visualize them as being connected to Source, and then I don't have to worry or have fearful thoughts about them anymore?

FEAR. Exactly!

EMILY. You seem to have two titles: Takes Action and Connected to Source. Of course, I don't know when I will ever be able to say I have fully integrated with Connected to Source.

FEAR. My dear Emily, you were never disconnected from Source. You only thought you were! Your use of *fully integrated* refers to when you are ready to acknowledge this as a true aspect of yourself. Do not be concerned about being totally connected to Source as Jesus was. That is a lifetime goal and will only frustrate you at this time.

EMILY. Thank you. Are you willing to join the team as Takes Action and Connected to Source?

TAKES ACTION AND CONNECTED TO SOURCE. We are ready to join the team. We have always been with you, almost from the beginning of your physical life.

EMILY. Welcome to the team! This was not as scary as I thought it would be, and in my mind, I see you smiling like a loving parent. Thank you very much.

After lunch, I get a yes that Beloved would like to dialogue, but I am unable to believe that Beloved would actually choose to dialogue with me, so I prepare for a short hike. However, curiosity soon has me back in my folding chair, ready to write. I call in my support team.

EMILY. Are you really ready and willing to dialogue with me, Beloved?

BELOVED. I have always been ready and willing to dialogue with you, dear Emily. It is you who is now ready and willing to talk with me. I am an aspect of you, after all.

EMILY. Yes, I keep forgetting that. You seem to be too lofty to be an aspect of mine. Remember the assignment you mentioned that was needed before we could continue—to sit daily and open myself to God's love? Was that for my own opening as well?

BELOVED. Yes, it was, and now you are ready and willing to continue.

EMILY. I guess I am. I just reread our dialogue from July 30, 2012, and you were encouraging. Are you now ready to join the team? Or maybe it is more accurate to ask if I am now ready, willing, and open to having you join the team, Beloved. Shall we do this?

BELOVED. It is my honor to join the team.

EMILY. I am honored as well. I feel you are fully integrated at this time. My heart is opening, and I feel a deep, contented joy. I am blessed and grateful to have you, Beloved, on the team. Actually, I feel awed and a little light-headed.

BELOVED. I bring a new vibration. Relax, and enjoy!

September 11, 2012

This morning, I investigate the bookstore at Breitenbush. Only one book appeals to me: *Unconditional Forgiveness* by Mary Hayes Grieco. I groan inside myself and walk around the bookstore a second time, but the results are the same. I buy the book. I begin my dialogues with Clarity after calling in my support team.

EMILY. Good morning, Clarity. Do you have comments for me?

CLARITY. Yes. Relax, and enjoy. You are being led to do some forgiveness work from your high school days. The new book will help.

Using my new book, *Unconditional Forgiveness*, I begin the eight-step process around my high school years. I realize how much the actions of a few individuals affected that time in my life. They were the primary reason I was alone and without a friend for three years. I discover a huge block of anger, and I let out my rage over spending three years of high school in bitter loneliness.

At the end of the process, I realize that I did receive some gifts from that experience. I became a much stronger person, and I learned

I could manage even if alone. It was not a pleasant experience, but I did it. Today this is one of my strengths, as I am easily able to travel by myself, and I thoroughly enjoy my own company.

I am now ready to continue my dialogues with a character trait identified through my inner-child work that I call Inability to Say No.

EMILY. I am now ready and willing to open a dialogue with Inability to Say No.

I feel uncomfortable, but I am willing to see what happens.

EMILY. Are you willing to dialogue with me?

INABILITY TO SAY NO. Yes. I am a legitimate aspect, and you have been using my services for most of your life—at least since you were two and a half years of age.

EMILY. Thank you. Do you have other comments to share? In my mind's eye, I see you say, "Humph," and you seem to be frustrated.

INABILITY TO SAY NO. It is just that I have served you so faithfully all this time, and I am only now being noticed.

EMILY. I appreciate your dedication, but I do not see how you have helped me. There must be a reason, or you would not have stayed so long. Please comment.

INABILITY TO SAY NO. You bet. There are many good reasons. I helped you survive in your childhood years; I helped you with many of your jobs; I helped you raise your two girls with little help from others; and I helped you care for your parents, not physically but emotionally, over the years, just to name a few.

EMILY. I see what you mean, and I am grateful. However, I don't seem to know how to say no to others or myself when too much is being asked of me. I am learning to set priorities better, and I realize I need to be able to disappoint others sometimes, but this does not come easily for me.

INABILITY TO SAY NO. When you get back home, do this: go off by yourself with a big piece of paper, your soft pastels, and the space to move around. Practice saying no the way you did not get to do when you were two and a half years old. That will take care of a huge backlog of not being able to say no to others. Please do this soon. You need to be able to get dirty with the pastels and make a lot of noise. Good luck.

EMILY. Thank you so much. I will do this. I am now ready and willing to dialogue with Anger. Are you ready and willing to dialogue with me?

ANGER. You are going to need the pastels for me also, but we can start now even without them. Yes, I am willing to dialogue with you. In fact, I think you have been afraid to talk to me for some time now.

EMILY. Well, that is true, but for some reason, I am calm at this moment. Maybe I am tired. I don't know.

ANGER. You do not have to be afraid of me, Emily. You were so terrified of any loud noises, shouting, or conflict when you were young that you totally shut me down for a long time. As an infant, you were able to express your anger openly, but that all stopped at two and a half, when you had a negative encounter with me. I am sorry that event took place, as a good dose of anger gets the adrenaline pumping, and things happen. I'm talking about anger being expressed. You could not help but have anger, but you kept it inside and never let anyone know, especially your thinking mind. You were afraid someone would not like you or love you. It is time to let go of that mode of behavior.

EMILY. Wow! This is totally different than I thought it would be. I was afraid to dialogue with you, as I thought I would have to shout and get angry, which meant I would need to be alone when I talked to you. Now you sound like Fear did yesterday—sort of like a helpful parent.

ANGER. There is nothing wrong with anger. It is an important feeling. It helps you decide things and take action, but it is not meant to be stuffed and not allowed to flow through the body. I do not agree with those who think anger is a bad emotion that should never be felt. There are not good or bad emotions; there are only freely flowing ones and stuffed ones.

EMILY. Thank you for sharing this wisdom. Do you have a positive title I need to discern at this time?

ANGER. *Discern* is an interesting word. I am pondering that.

EMILY. I will give you some time. Here are some words that come to my mind: *prioritizing, boundaries, safe boundaries,* and *secure boundaries.*

Suddenly, I feel tired. I am learning that often, resistance equals being tired. A raven flies overhead, and I hear its powerful wingbeats. Is this a message?

EMILY. More words have come to me: *honest, noble, at ease, peaceful, calm,* and *integrity.*

ANGER. I like *integrity.* Being honest and in your integrity allows emotions to flow. How do you really feel? Isn't that what integrity is all about?

EMILY. My dictionary says *integrity* equals *honesty.* I have a feeling this means going inside myself to identify what I am really feeling and then allowing the feeling to express itself appropriately, either aloud or through art, writing, or making sounds—all without being ashamed or embarrassed that I am having a feeling.

I have the thought that I often feel angry when I think I have been slighted or not understood by others. Inside myself, I am furious, but I do not know how to express this anger appropriately, so it stays inside. Maybe this issue does have to do with integrity. At times like that, I do not feel valued as a person who can think or have an opinion, which makes me feel angry. I am confused.

ANGER. We need to back up here.

EMILY. Yes, I would like you to join the team as Integrity. Are you willing at this time?

ANGER. I am honored to join the team as Integrity. I do see that you have some sorting out to do about who you really are and whether or not you have been devalued or just have not been heard. As a means of clarification, it is appropriate to stop a conversation with anyone to ask the person to repeat back what he or she thinks you just said. Try it sometime. I think it would be helpful. Then you can save anger for urgent needs, but first, see what is behind the anger. You might find it is something different. Anger is an overused emotion—whether it is stuck or flowing.

I find this all amazing.

EMILY. Thank you again for your wise comments. Welcome to the team, Integrity. It is an honor to have you with me.

I do a welcome ceremony and drop a small leaf into a tiny stream of water. As I drop the leaf, it flips in the air and lands on the stream bank—very much in its integrity. I leave it where it landed.

It is getting dark, but I have an urge to construct a small stick shelter over a piece of moss and place a small, flat piece of bark on the shelter. This is a shelter and a nest for Baby Emily. I feel strongly that she needs a shelter and a nest at this time. It feels good to give these to her.

September 12, 2012

This morning, I do some deep forgiveness work before calling in my support team. I get a yes to begin my dialogues with Beloved.

EMILY. Beloved, do you have comments for me?

BELOVED. Well done! I can feel your heart expanding. Do not be cautious about this. You are opening to receive the gifts of the universe. Know that you need never feel alone again. You are always loved and always were. You just didn't know it. I love you.

EMILY. I love you! I am so grateful! I think I am ready and willing to dialogue with People Pleaser. Are you ready and willing?

PEOPLE PLEASER. Well, I suppose so. This is all a little silly, you know. You have been skirting around me now for months, and finally, you are ready to "tackle talking to me." Those were the words you thought and did not write down, were they not?

EMILY. Well, yes, they were. That is my people-pleasing tendency. Do you have comments?

PEOPLE PLEASER. You might not be liked by others without me. You might be alone without me. You might be unhappy without me.

EMILY. I am learning that I can be alone and still be happy. I am also not as needy for others to like me as I used to be. I am getting the feeling I have dialogued with someone quite like you before. You remind me of Perfectionist, who chose the new title of Organized. I sense you are different, even though you help me to accomplish similar things. Is this true?

PEOPLE PLEASER. Yes, we are different. I have nothing to do with being organized. No, that is certainly not me. I have to do with bowing, scraping, taking the last piece, not feeling good about yourself, and doing for others first at all costs. I do not think this is something you are going to stop doing easily.

EMILY. Thank you for sharing. Are you connected to Peace at Any Price?

PEOPLE PLEASER. That is my main motto. Do you like it? Well, I'm not really asking, because honesty is not part of my thing, and I am not pleased with your joining up with Integrity yesterday. That will put a real crimp in my style. You will have to make some mighty big changes if you really want to integrate with Integrity. Did you even think about all the repercussions for that one small act? Well, it was a big act!

EMILY. I sense you are upset. Please tell me about more of your positive aspects.

PEOPLE PLEASER. I already told you all you need to know.

EMILY. I was just trying to get an idea of why you have been with me for so long.

PEOPLE PLEASER. How could people living together ever hope to get along if they're honest all the time? Why, there would be constant war.

EMILY. I see. You do not think honesty can bring up loving comments as well.

PEOPLE PLEASER. If it suits the purpose.

EMILY. I am at a loss as to how to proceed, but I do feel we are having a fine, open conversation for the first time. I am pleased we are both speaking so openly and frankly.

PEOPLE PLEASER. I always like to say what I think will please, but you are bringing out an uncomfortable segment of my role. I am not really the bad guy. I just can't see how you are ever going to get along with others if you do not try to please them.

EMILY. How about just being who I am, letting them be who they are, and accepting that? I am even beginning to work on accepting myself.

PEOPLE PLEASER. Humbug. All this openness stuff—makes me nauseated. I think I have to go for now.

EMILY. All right. I am glad we got a start, though. I have been afraid to talk to you, but like all the others, you are a unique character.

PEOPLE PLEASER. You can say that again. I am a stubborn one too!

EMILY. That's all right. Your openness is refreshing.

PEOPLE PLEASER. No, the last thing I want is to be open. How did you get that word for me? I am the secret—the skeleton in the closet, if you please—and openness is not one of my traits.

EMILY. I just meant how well you have been explaining yourself. I understand your role, and I have been puzzled by you for a long time. I also feel I can dialogue with you more in the future.

PEOPLE PLEASER. If you must.

EMILY. Let's wait and see.

PEOPLE PLEASER. You are the one getting me to be so open. I do not usually discuss my methods. I keep them well hidden from the light of exposure.

EMILY. You are even charming. I'm getting to like you.

PEOPLE PLEASER. Humph! Enough for today.

EMILY. All right. Bye for now.

PEOPLE PLEASER. Always have to have the last word. That does not get you points with me.

I smile.

EMILY. Bye.

I close my amazing retreat at Breitenbush astounded over all that has occurred. I don't know what is happening to me, but it all feels beneficial. I am curious to see what will happen next.

Chart of Aspects as of September 12, 2012

New Name	Previous Name	Date First Noted	Date Fully Integrated
Tenacity	Rigid Taskmaster	4-7-12	5-8-12
Courage	Stern Enforcer	4-7-12	5-8-12
Flexible	Saboteur	6-4-12	
Balanced	Defective	6-12-12	8-11-12
Beloved	Unlovable	6-12-12	9-10-12
Precious	Unworthy	6-12-12	
Clarity	Overwhelmed and Confused	6-20-12	9-5-12
Conscience	Guilt	6-20-12	8-3-12
Organized	Perfectionist	7-9-12	8-13-12
Let It Be	Judge's Eye	7-13-12	7-13-12
Self-Esteem	Sick Hospital Patient	7-25-12	
Safety Team and Security Force	Safety Team and Security Force	8-3-12	8-3-12
Intuition	Super-Responsible One	8-6-12	8-6-12
Joy	Sadness	8-6-12	8-6-12
Strength	Inadequate	8-11-12	8-11-12
Acceptance	Pity	8-27-12	9-5-12
Playful	Shy One	8-27-12	8-27-12

Takes Action Connected to Source	Fear	9-10-12	9-10-12
	Inability to Say No	9-11-12	
Integrity	Anger	9-11-12	9-11-12
	People Pleaser	9-12-12	

Chapter 7

Your Body Is Wise
and Can Help You

September 21, 2012

I CALL IN MY support team and reread my dialogue with Inability to Say No from September 11, 2012. Last night, I had two frustrating dreams, and I wonder if there is a connection.

EMILY. Are you ready and willing to dialogue with me, Inability to Say No?

INABILTY TO SAY NO. No, as you have not done the assignment I gave you more than a week ago. And yes, that is why I am frustrated.

EMILY. I will do the assignment right now.

I take out my soft pastels and a large piece of paper. Then I pretend to be my two-and-a-half-year-old self and practice saying no.

I write the word *no* on the page over and over as I shout, "No!" Then the words change to *stop*, *don't*, and *not*.

EMILY. This is amazing! Do you have comments now?

INABILTY TO SAY NO. Well, it was a good start, but you need to do more.

EMILY. All right. I will continue on another day. May I do that?

INABILTY TO SAY NO. Yes, I think you have done a good job today, but don't wait too long. This is helping your family as well. I think you had that insight during the *no* process, correct?

EMILY. Yes, I did. I am glad for your confirmation. Thank you.

INABILTY TO SAY NO. I mean, this is really going to help your family a lot—past, present, and future—not to mention how much it will help you. Even if you do not have the need to say no right now, you need to do this for all the years when you were not able to say no.

EMILY. Again, thank you. I appreciate you.

INABILTY TO SAY NO. I am glad also. I love you.

EMILY. I love you as well.

Five nights ago, I had a puzzling dream called Troubled Girl. It in, I met a girl in an orphanage. She was trying to seem older than she was, and other children didn't like her, but I still liked her. At the end, I saw her dressed up nicely and phoning her aunt. I was glad she at least had a relative to call.

Then, last night, I had a dream in which I got so frustrated with two young women that I ended up rubbing a wet floor mop in each of their faces. At the end, I asked their names, which were Snit and Snat. I decide to explore these two dreams.

EMILY. Are you ready to dialogue with me, Snit and Snat?

SNIT AND SNAT. I suppose so.

EMILY. Thank you. I am sorry about the wet mop in the face last night. I know now that you are aspects of me, and I don't know why I was so frustrated. Do you have any comments for me?

SNIT AND SNAT. Sort of. We are appearing now because you did a lot of work at your Breitenbush retreat, but it did not really include us.

EMILY. All right. Who are you, and what do you represent? Are you connected to the Troubled Girl dream of five nights ago?

SNIT AND SNAT. We do not like multiple questions, but if you insist. We represent an unconscious part of you. We have to do with rebellion. You have lived a controlled life, and now you are skirting around some new, potentially dangerous and transformative ideas. You are shaking up how you do things and changing your beliefs. This is good, but it might feel unsettling.

EMILY. Yes, it does, hence the wet mop in the face. I'm sorry about that.

SNIT AND SNAT. Well, you are doing it to yourself, you know.

EMILY. Oh yes. I keep forgetting that you are aspects of me and not some other person or being. These dialogues are always a surprise.

SNIT AND SNAT. Good. They should be. You have never contacted us before, and we want to dialogue with you. Now, back to the

73

other question regarding Troubled Girl. Yes, we are related. She went first to try to get your attention, and we think it worked.

EMILY. Yes, it did. I am curious and a little concerned.

SNIT AND SNAT. That has to do with your discomfort with rebellion. You do not like to be different from the people around you. You are used to giving up on who you are and what your truth is in order to be like other people, hoping they'll like you. None of this is necessary, as you are loved anyway for who you are.

EMILY. Thank you for this intriguing information.

September 28, 2012

Today I had lunch with a friend, and we had a deep conversation about life and death. Now I am at the studio, and I call in my support team.

EMILY. I am now ready and willing to dialogue with Beloved. Are you ready and willing to dialogue with me?

BELOVED. Of course I am. You are much loved, dear Emily. Do not be afraid to connect with your aspects. And you are right about there being no death.

EMILY. I am tired. Do you have any special comments for me, or do I need to go home to rest and do this another time?

BELOVED. Your energy is a bit low at this time. Just sit quietly and feel my love for a few more minutes.

EMILY. I will do that part, but I am too tired to continue. I'm sorry. I will be back another day.

October 3, 2012

At the studio, I connect with my support team and get a reluctant yes to dialogue with Self-Esteem.

EMILY. I now open a dialogue with Self-Esteem. Do you have comments for me?

SELF-ESTEEM. Please reread our other dialogue to refresh yourself, and yes, I have comments.

EMILY. I see you are not fully integrated, and you gave me an assignment on July 25, 2012. You were the Sick Hospital Patient when we first met. I said I would get back to you in a week, and now it is October. I know I was not ready to accept you at that time, but I am curious to hear what you have to say now. Please comment.

SELF-ESTEEM. Well, your work on my assignment to hug me, say you love me, and feel the divine within has been really helping me. I appreciate your participation.

EMILY. I think it is helping me. I am still getting used to the concept that I am actually talking to a part of myself. Please continue.

SELF-ESTEEM. I don't know what to say. I am glowing with pride, joy, love, and appreciation.

EMILY. I am thrilled to learn this. We have done enormous healing, especially this summer. Do you have another title to go by, or do you like Self-Esteem?

SELF-ESTEEM. I really like the concept. See what words come to you, though, just to be sure.

EMILY. All right. I sense the words *proud, pride, content, glowing, honest, self-assured,* and *confident.* Do any of these capture your fancy?

SELF-ESTEEM. Oh, I like the name Self-Assured the best, even better than Self-Esteem, which could be positive or negative.

EMILY. Self-Assured it is. Are you ready to join the team?

SELF-ASSURED. I am honored to join the team. Thank you.

I take a short nap and then am ready to continue.

EMILY. I open a dialogue with Joy. Do you have any comments for me?

JOY. Please reread our last conversation, just as Self-Esteem, now Self-Assured, suggested.

EMILY. You mean you are all listening in on the others' dialogues?

JOY. Of course. We are all parts of the whole you.

EMILY. Amazing! I am still learning about that.

JOY. Yes, isn't it great?

EMILY. It is truly a joy!

JOY. Tee-hee!

EMILY. What comments do you have for me?

JOY. Well, I have not seen much of you lately. I know being in joy is a new thing for you, but I am patient—tenacious, in fact.

EMILY. Good. Yes, we have Tenacity on the team. Please continue.

JOY. Do you see how you do some dialoguing, get tired, rest for a few minutes, and then are filled with more energy and pep? Well, this is a good way to notice what your body needs at any given moment. This is good information for you. Your body is wise, and it can help you to help your body. We are all in this lifetime together.

EMILY. Amazing! So you are not just about being silly and fluff?

JOY. Oh no. I am much deeper than that. In fact, I am close to your core. I am extremely important for you and for our well-being.

EMILY. I am still amazed and inspired. I am getting the urge to move and dance. Is that you?

JOY. It is! Let's dance!

I dance around the studio space, moving with joyous abandon.

EMILY. Yes, this feels so good!

JOY. I know we are going to folk dancing tonight, and I want to be ready!

EMILY. Me too. Thank you. I now open a dialogue with Inability to Say No. Do you have comments for me?

INABILITY TO SAY NO. You need to continue using the soft pastels and paper while saying no as a two-and-a-half-year-old and then move up in years like you did the last time. Eventually, our talks will become easier, and you will not want to put me off.

EMILY. You are all so honest.

INABILITY TO SAY NO. As aspects of you, we would never tell you anything but the real truth, even if you do not want to hear it.

EMILY. Actually, I have been noticing that, and I am relieved to hear you say it. Thank you.

I use my soft pastels and paper as I say no in all the ways I can think of. I fill one side of a large page and then fold it in half and continue until I can't fold anymore.

EMILY. It is exhilarating to say no! Thank you for encouraging me, Inability to Say No.

INABILITY TO SAY NO. I thought you would appreciate this exercise. I am glad you are listening to me. I would like to see you strong in the ability to say no.

EMILY. Oh, I would too.

INABILITY TO SAY NO. Keep trying!

October 6, 2012

I take part in a group retreat at the Oregon coast, during which I happen to draw the card for archetype magician. This is amazing, as one of the attributes of this archetype is transformation, and I have certainly been doing a great deal of transforming lately.

October 12, 2012

I am back at the studio and get a yes to dialogue with People Pleaser. I reread my only dialogue with this aspect, which was on September 12, 2012. It was quite a conversation.

EMILY. Are you willing to dialogue with me, People Pleaser?

PEOPLE PLEASER. I certainly am. You never know what I am going to say, do you?

EMILY. No, I do not, but that keeps this interesting.

PEOPLE PLEASER. I want to comment on the archetype magician, which you chose to work with at the retreat. This is an extremely powerful archetype. If you make full use of archetype magician, I will indeed be able to do some real transforming. That is what you've wanted all along, is it not? Transformation. That is what you came to Earth at this time to accomplish, is it not? Well, I think so, and I know that working with this archetype will be an exciting and challenging ride. I like challenges.

EMILY. I am not sure about you, People Pleaser. You are the only aspect I do not feel I can trust, as you told me honesty was not your thing. Please comment.

PEOPLE PLEASER. Oh, I am honest with you at all times. I meant that I don't think you can keep peace at any price and still be honest with all others.

EMILY. Thank you for the clarification. I feel that I am an honest person, but I do avoid speaking if I think it will cause conflict of any kind. Please continue.

PEOPLE PLEASER. You are going to have to develop a way to have more intestinal fortitude if you are going to work with transformation.

EMILY. How can I develop more intestinal fortitude?

PEOPLE PLEASER. Be more aware of what is going on in your life, inside your body, and all around you. I see you just reacting on a whim to whatever feeling sweeps over you. Instead, stop. Be aware. You do not have to let emotions push you around. It ticks me off when you do that—and you do it a lot.

EMILY. I see this as my people-pleaser trait, but now I hear you talking in a favorable way about transformation. Will you help me transform?

PEOPLE PLEASER. That I will. This is exciting for me.

EMILY. What else can I do?

PEOPLE PLEASER. Learn more about archetype magician for a start. And I like the way you are stepping out and signing yourself up for new and different experiences. It's time for me to go for now.

EMILY. Thank you. I am now ready to open a dialogue with Self-Assured. Do you have any comments?

SELF-ASSURED. I am quiet and calm at this time. This is a change for me, as I tend to go to the anxious side. I got a bit anxious last night at your class when you could sense you were not saying what one participant needed to hear. I want you to know I am proud of the way you handled and, yes, transformed that situation. And during the night, you realized that a good teacher can let others be the ones with the best answers. It does not have to be you. This will free you up to be more self-assured, have more fun, and lighten up on yourself.

EMILY. Thank you for these comments, and I appreciate the acknowledgment. I am still amazed at this whole process. I am now ready and willing to dialogue with Connected to Source. Well, I think I am. I somehow feel like I should be able to hear clear guidance telling me things like "Do this now," but I do not hear this clear direction. Does this mean I am not connected to Source? And yes, I am now ready to dialogue. Please comment.

CONNECTED TO SOURCE. Oh, Emily, you do not have to hear words in your head to be connected to Source. You have recently been following your own hunches and beginning to tune in to your own magnificent guidance system. This is connection to Source. Source is not going to dictate the actions of your life to you. As you become more aligned with your own higher self, the inner knowing will come to you.

EMILY. Thank you. I often feel that others will look at my hunches as silly and unreasonable. Can you help me?

CONNECTED TO SOURCE. You are just beginning to work in this huge and amazing area. Have patience, relax, and enjoy the ride. Remember, you are an eternal being, and there is no real right or wrong. Let others take care of themselves in their own ways. It is fine to follow your hunches. You do not need to explain yourself to anyone. Just be you.

EMILY. Thank you. I feel much better.

Chart of Aspects as of October 12, 2012

New Name	Previous Name	Date First Noted	Date Fully Integrated
Tenacity	Rigid Taskmaster	4-7-12	5-8-12
Courage	Stern Enforcer	4-7-12	5-8-12
Flexible	Saboteur	6-4-12	
Balanced	Defective	6-12-12	8-11-12
Beloved	Unlovable	6-12-12	9-10-12
Precious	Unworthy	6-12-12	
Clarity	Overwhelmed and Confused	6-20-12	9-5-12
Conscience	Guilt	6-20-12	8-3-12
Organized	Perfectionist	7-9-12	8-13-12
Let It Be	Judge's Eye	7-13-12	7-13-12
Self-Esteem Self-Assured	Sick Hospital Patient Self-Esteem	7-25-12 10-3-12	10-3-12
Safety Team and Security Force	Safety Team and Security Force	8-3-12	8-3-12
Intuition	Super-Responsible One	8-6-12	8-6-12
Joy	Sadness	8-6-12	8-6-12
Strength	Inadequate	8-11-12	8-11-12
Acceptance	Pity	8-27-12	9-5-12

Playful	Shy One	8-27-12	8-27-12
Takes Action and Connected to Source	Fear	9-10-12	9-10-12
	Inability to Say No	9-11-12	
Integrity	Anger	9-11-12	9-11-12
	People Pleaser	9-12-12	
	Snit and Snat	9-21-12	

Chapter 8

Birthing the New Earth

October 28–30, 2012

I AM NOURISHED BY retreats in nature, so I take myself to a heated cabin at Silver Falls State Park. I spend three days walking out in nature and doing forgiveness work in the cabin. I use Mary Hayes Grieco's *Unconditional Forgiveness* book to do deep forgiveness work on anyone and anything that comes to mind. I feel liberated at the end of each process.

November 2–4, 2012

I attend a Tom Kenyon sound healing event in Seattle.

November 6, 2012

I connect with my support team.

EMILY. Are you ready and willing to dialogue with me, Snit and Snat?

SNIT AND SNAT. We certainly are ready and willing. We sense you are not comfortable with talking to us, though.

EMILY. You are correct. I just reread our first dialogue of September 21, 2012, and saw that you have to do with rebellion, transformation, and doing things differently from others. This is unsettling for me. Please comment.

SNIT AND SNAT. Oh, we would love to talk. We are your aspects who walk on the wild side—and did we ever walk at the Tom Kenyon sound healing seminar! We are pleased you took us to that event. It was great and transformative for us all. Thank you!

EMILY. I am glad you are pleased. I did the best I could to let go of control and allow as much as possible to unfold.

SNIT AND SNAT. We see that, and we acknowledge you for your courage, tenacity, and willingness to try new things.

EMILY. Thank you. I love your encouragement. Now, I do want to have a new title for you. Comments?

SNIT AND SNAT. Oh yes, we want a new title—something adventurous.

EMILY. I like that—Adventurous. Shall that be your new title? Or Open? Wild One? Rebellious? What is your favorite?

SNIT AND SNAT. We like Adventurous.

EMILY. So be it. Are you ready and willing to join the team, Adventurous?

ADVENTUROUS. Yes! This is exciting! We have been with you a long time but have not been acknowledged for quite a while.

EMILY. Welcome to the team, Adventurous! I am now ready and willing to dialogue with Beloved. Do you have comments for me?

BELOVED. We feel your apprehension. Do not be concerned about talking to us. Remember, we are here only to love and support you in all you do and seek. We enjoy that you felt our deep, unconditional love many times at the Tom Kenyon event. You are so loved.

EMILY. Thank you so much. I did bask in your love at the event. It was all so new. Thank you again. Do you have more comments?

BELOVED. We would like you to talk to Precious soon. Remember all the references Tom Kenyon made to feeling worthy? Those were for you as well as the others. After all the marvelous forgiveness work you have been doing, do you feel how your body is now starting to feel lighter?

EMILY. Well, maybe I do. I am not used to having a lighter body, and you do not mean physical mass, do you?

BELOVED. No, we mean your light, which is beginning to shine as you release the dark layers of judgment, fear, and worry over what you think others might be thinking. Mostly, we see your judgment of self and others leaving, and we encourage you to keep doing the forgiveness work. The technique from the book you were led to is good for you.

EMILY. Thank you so much. I am now ready and willing to dialogue with Precious. At least I think I am. I am a bit tired but will keep going anyway. Yes, I am ready and willing to dialogue. Do you have comments for me?

PRECIOUS. I am always ready and willing to dialogue with you, dear Emily. You are my beloved child, in whom I am well pleased.

EMILY. Thank you.

I shed some tears.

EMILY. I am trying on this feeling of being worthy of God's love. I am a little afraid that what I did at the Tom Kenyon event was too far out there.

PRECIOUS. Oh, Emily, do not worry so about needing to be right or only doing the so-called right thing. You can't get it wrong! Life is all an incredible experiment.

EMILY. I am not sure I like being part of an experiment.

PRECIOUS. Oh, you wanted to be in the experiment of birthing the new earth. You just forgot. That is all. Yes, this is what evolution of life is! It is all a grand experiment because it hasn't been done exactly this way ever before. How exciting! That is why it is so grand. Now, back to you and being worthy. Do you remember when I said you will integrate with me when you allow it to happen? I am always ready and willing to integrate with you. It is your choice. Are you now ready?

EMILY. Well, I think I might be.

PRECIOUS. Go inside to see what you see and feel what you feel, but remember, you now have Adventurous with you, and you just learned there is no need to concern yourself with getting it right.

EMILY. A few months ago, you gave me the assignment to say, "I am worthy of God's love, and I am precious in God's sight." At that time, I felt so unworthy. I have been doing your assignment, though, and now I feel fine integrating with you. Yes, I feel completely calm and honored with this entire idea. In fact, I am surprised I did not always feel this way. I can't remember not feeling this way. Please integrate with me, Precious, and be on the team.

PRECIOUS. I am honored to be a part of the team.

EMILY. I can hardly believe this. Welcome to the team, Precious. Is this an example of divine timing?

PRECIOUS. A perfect example. We are all smiling and sending our love to our precious Emily.

EMILY. Thank you so much. I am honored!

I remember that Beloved and Precious often use *I* and *we* interchangeably, as they are a small group (see chapter 3).

It is incredible to be present at the unfolding of each aspect through these dialogues. I can never guess what I will hear or what will happen.

November 11, 2012

I believe there is a connection between emotions and illness in the body. For several days now, I have had the urge to do this, and today I have the courage to begin. I use the self-forgiveness technique from *Unconditional Forgiveness* to forgive myself for having to go through the treatment for right breast cancer. This is huge for me, and I realize it is time to let go of my burden of guilt over everything involved, despite the fact that my life is much better in all respects than it was before my diagnosis. I also realize I am not through with this topic, but for today, I feel complete.

November 12, 2012

I awaken with this insight: "I allow my aspects into my heart, and I feel my heart opening to allow my aspects to return to me." I know this is one of my next steps: to allow the integration of each aspect.

November 19, 2012

Even though it was a stretch for me, I felt led to participate in a recent prayer event. Now I feel like a total failure at my first attempt to do healing prayer for others. On a hunch, I ask if I have an aspect called High Judge, and I get a yes. I call in my support team.

EMILY. Are you ready and willing to dialogue with me, High Judge?

HIGH JUDGE. I certainly am.

EMILY. Thank you. Can you please tell me about yourself and what you do for me?

HIGH JUDGE. I am a moral-issue type of judge, as in the rightness or wrongness of something.

EMILY. Thank you. I feel that you are hard on me and almost impossible to please. Do you have comments?

HIGH JUDGE. Well, I do have high standards. In fact, I like the title High Judge. It suits me well. Being joyful is not one of my goals.

EMILY. That is helpful. Would you be willing to consider the possibility that we could have high standards and still live in joy?

HIGH JUDGE. That is not something I have ever entertained. I will consider it at this time. I do not like this topic. Do you have another question?

EMILY. Yes, I do. It has to do with the Abraham material in the book *Ask and It Is Given* by Esther and Jerry Hicks, which says I have an inner being who only thinks positive thoughts about me and whatever I do. You are making it difficult for me to hear that voice. Please comment.

HIGH JUDGE. Well, I am certainly not this inner being who goes on and on about airy-fairy stuff that may or may not be true. I am telling the real story.

EMILY. Yes, you might be, but I am in the process of rewriting my own real story and transforming it into one with joy and beauty instead of always being in fear of not getting it right.

HIGH JUDGE. There you go, off on that flaky stuff. I like to keep things in reality and what I know to be true about us. I am not comfortable with all this change stuff either.

EMILY. I sense some fear coming up for you. May I hold you?

HIGH JUDGE. Well, it is not proper, but I would like to be held.

EMILY. I am holding you tightly to myself.

I am frightened by this part of me called High Judge. I do EFT tapping and make my fear sounds to release the fear. I suddenly feel calmer and am able to relax. The word *compassion* is strong for me, and then I feel grace and compassion sweep over my body.

EMILY. I feel much better now. Are you an aspect who would like to be called Compassion rather than High Judge?

HIGH JUDGE. I would really like to be Compassion. I am like some of the other aspects that will need to be learned.

EMILY. Would you please join the team and help me learn self-compassion?

HIGH JUDGE. It is a big request, but I think it is easier than joy.

EMILY. No problem. I have an aspect called Joy, so you do not have to be concerned about that. No, I need you to be Self-Compassion. I think once I have more self-compassion, it will naturally expand to compassion for others. Will you join the team as Self-Compassion?

HIGH JUDGE. Now that you put it that way, yes, I am willing to join as Self-Compassion.

EMILY. Thank you so much. I welcome you, Self-Compassion, to the team!

December 3, 2012

I have just returned from participating in Sonia Choquette's Ask Your Guides workshop. It was amazing! I just did it. Something must be changing within me, as I always thought such a workshop would be impossible, but now I have just participated in one. I connect with my support team and proceed.

EMILY. I am now ready to open a dialogue with Self-Assured, who only recently integrated. Do you have comments for me?

SELF-ASSURED. I am pleased to be a part of the team. I am grateful for the way we opened ourselves to guidance over the last two days at the workshop. This was wonderful and inspiring. Thank you for attending this event.

EMILY. I appreciate that you are pleased and that you appreciate my efforts too. I appreciate you!

SELF-ASSURED. I am just beaming!

EMILY. I can feel you beaming with joy and the satisfaction of a job well done. Do you have any more to say?

SELF-ASSURED. Yes, I want you to note how this feels and consider that this could be your normal, natural state of being. Why be any less than pleased with yourself and who you are?

EMILY. Wow! What a great concept. Yes, it does feel good, and well, why not make this my normal way to be? Thank you so much! Anything else?

SELF-ASSURED. Yes, I am glad you caught yourself last night at dinner and stopped telling yourself that you were not as good as the other three women at the table. You have your own gifts, and they are not the same as others' gifts. Please do not judge and compare yourself so much. I know this is a learning process for you, but your whole team is here to support and encourage you.

EMILY. Thank you so much. I now open a dialogue with Playful. Do you have something to share with me?

PLAYFUL. I am honored. Do you remember how you danced and moved with great abandon yesterday at the workshop? That is a step in being flexible. This is how you will learn to open yourself more fully to us, your aspects; your higher self; and more. Why not do some movement now instead of the nap you are considering?

EMILY. Oh, this is new. Well, okay, I'll give it a go.

I dance around the room as I did at the workshop.

EMILY. That was great!

PLAYFUL. Yes, it was. Please consider doing this more often. You know, you are used to being proper and organized. You are missing out on the joy of being in this body and in this life. Please lighten up for the good of us all!

EMILY. Thank you for sharing all of this with me. I appreciate your reminding me. And I do not need a nap right now after all! Do you have more to say?

PLAYFUL. No, but the playful part is maybe the most important part for you at this time. It is way more important than you are giving it credit for. This is not a mild suggestion. This is an urgent need!

EMILY. Yes, I am feeling that. This is a huge shift for me. Please help me.

PLAYFUL. That is why I am here.

December 5, 2012

Today in my session with Georgie, she gives me some observations. She says these aspects developed in my childhood. For example, my three-year-old self developed certain aspects to go along with the life experiences at that age. Now, as I continue my inner-child work, I am uncovering more aspects. She feels this is a unique way of doing inner-child work, and she has never heard of anything like it before. I ponder her comments. They feel true for me.

December 12, 2012

Last night, I had a dream I called Black Woman. In it, I was in a dark warehouse with my daughters, and we found a black female lying on the dirt floor. I thought she was dead. I kicked at her side once and stepped back. We watched as she started to get up, and we realized she was not dead after all. I decide to explore this dream character, and I call in my support team.

EMILY. I wish to dialogue with the black woman from my dream last night. Are you willing to dialogue with me?

BLACK WOMAN IN DREAM. Yes, I am, and it was more than a nudge you gave me. You thought I was dead, didn't you?

EMILY. Yes, I did, and I am sorry I kicked you. Who are you?

BLACK WOMAN IN DREAM. I am Trust and Faith—trust in yourself, which becomes faith in yourself.

EMILY. I see. Thank you. Why did you come to me last night?

BLACK WOMAN IN DREAM. Because you really need me at this time.

EMILY. I suppose I do. I just looked over my list of aspects, and I do not see one that matches you, except maybe Self-Assured. Are you part of Self-Assured?

BLACK WOMAN IN DREAM. Self-Assured, being more alive within you, will be the result of trust and faith in yourself. You need to start with trust and faith in yourself. You are just beginning to take the steps of defining who you are and what some of your abilities are. Please investigate this further, and do not be afraid to ask for help from your aspects.

EMILY. Thank you so much. I sense I need to do something before you will integrate.

BLACK WOMAN IN DREAM. Yes, you do. You will need to affirm the following: "I now trust my faith in myself to make the best choices for me." Then you will need to explore and practice. The trust and faith will only come through experience. Relax, and enjoy. This is a grand opening for you!

December 18, 2012

In my session with Georgie today, she asks if I've had any health issues this year. I laugh, as my health was my primary reason for doing inner-child work in the first place. I did have one easily treated urinary tract infection in the fall due to taking a bath in scented Epsom salts, but over this past year, my life has expanded exponentially, and I am exploring a world I did not even know existed: my own unknown inner self. I am so excited about all I am experiencing that I forgot about any medical needs.

I am grateful for that nudge a year ago to do the inner-child work or face health issues. In my wildest dreams, I never could have predicted the results.

Chart of Aspects as of December 18, 2012

New Name	Previous Name	Date First Noted	Date Fully Integrated
Tenacity	Rigid Taskmaster	4-7-12	5-8-12
Courage	Stern Enforcer	4-7-12	5-8-12
Flexible	Saboteur	6-4-12	
Balanced	Defective	6-12-12	8-11-12
Beloved	Unlovable	6-12-12	9-10-12
Precious	Unworthy	6-12-12	11-6-12
Clarity	Overwhelmed and Confused	6-20-12	9-5-12
Conscience	Guilt	6-20-12	8-3-12
Organized	Perfectionist	7-9-12	8-13-12
Let It Be	Judge's Eye	7-13-12	7-13-12
Self-Esteem Self-Assured	Sick Hospital Patient Self-Esteem	7-25-12 10-3-12	10-3-12
Safety Team and Security Force	Safety Team and Security Force	8-3-12	8-3-12
Intuition	Super-Responsible One	8-6-12	8-6-12
Joy	Sadness	8-6-12	8-6-12
Strength	Inadequate	8-11-12	8-11-12
Acceptance	Pity	8-27-12	9-5-12

Playful	Shy One	8-27-12	8-27-12
Takes Action and Connected to Source	Fear	9-10-12	9-10-12
	Inability to Say No	9-11-12	
Integrity	Anger	9-11-12	9-11-12
	People Pleaser	9-12-12	
Adventurous	Snit and Snat	9-21-12	11-6-12
Self-Compassion	High Judge	11-19-12	11-19-12
Trust and Faith in Self	Black Woman in Dream	12-12-12	

SMILE

Chapter 9

Self-Care Starts with Extreme Self-Compassion

January 6, 2013

I CALL IN MY support team and ask if Beloved is ready and willing to dialogue with me.

BELOVED. You are not sure if you are actually looking forward to my comments, are you?

EMILY. You are right. I feel a twinge of unworthiness and a little fear, but please continue.

BELOVED. We are the part of you who showers you with love at all times. We love that you are learning to open up and allow your cells to resonate with the unconditional love and light of the divine. Please do this daily until it becomes natural for you. This is amazingly helpful to your body. We love you!

EMILY. Thank you for your wise words. I am now ready and willing to open a dialogue with Joy, despite the fact that I do not feel any joy at this time.

JOY. That is because you keep thinking joy is the quality of having it all together and knowing all the right answers before you let yourself experience joy in your life. Remember, you can't get it wrong, so why not enjoy the process? The journey is what it is all about. We are here now to remind you of that. You may bask in joy even in the darkest of times, when you really get the part about life being a learning and growing experience and not about who is doing life perfectly. There is your life, and however you live it is perfect. Thrill each day at the fact that you are in your lovely physical body and able to breath in and out, feel love for your cells, and bask in the glow of divine light. That is all I have to share at this time. The more you focus on this, the more you will feel joy in your life.

EMILY. I am amazed at the wisdom coming through on this quiet day. Thank you, Joy, for sharing. Now, are you ready and willing to dialogue with me, Playful?

PLAYFUL. You bet! We have a few minutes to sing and move about. Let's do it!

EMILY. Yes, it is great to move and sing. I thank you for helping me to feel exuberant!

PLAYFUL. Now, why don't you use your new colored markers to make some playful drawings on the first page of this book? You know, the page you are always meaning to use for some artistic expression and never get around to doing.

EMILY. Fantastic idea!

I use my colored markers and create fun images in my notebook.

PLAYFUL. You are so serious. I have got to do something about this situation.

I laugh.

EMILY. Thank you so much, and the colors flowed so wonderfully.

PLAYFUL. Don't worry; I will never give up on you!

January 14–15, 2013

Fascinated by what is happening with these dialogues, I take myself on another personal retreat to a private heated cabin at Silver Falls State Park. This is an ideal location, as I can make as much noise as I need to without concern for neighbors. I decide to release the burden of unresolved anger. As I believe there is an emotional component to illness, this feels like an important step for me at this time. Using the book *Unconditional Forgiveness*, I do the forgiveness process on as many people as time allows.

During these processes, however, an intriguing thing happens: I realize I need to do self-forgiveness. I need to forgive my lovely body for all the anger, rage, fear, and other negative emotions trapped inside her for all these years. I took the first step in self-forgiveness last November (see chapter 8). It is time to continue.

Then another idea comes to me. I decide to see if my mental and emotional selves will ask forgiveness of my physical body. After all, these are also parts of myself, so why not try to dialogue with them? I have never read or heard about anything like this before. I am completely led by my intuition. I venture into uncharted territory as I call in my support team and proceed.

EMILY. Dear Physical Body, I realize you got hurt in all of the above ways with anger, rage, fear, and other negative emotions trapped inside my body. Are you willing to dialogue with me at this time?

I hear nothing.

EMILY. Dear Mental Body, are you willing to dialogue with me at this time?

MENTAL BODY. Yes, I am willing.

EMILY. Thank you. Emotional Body, are you willing to dialogue with me at this time?

EMOTIONAL BODY. Yes, but I am sad about this.

EMILY. I know, but let's keep going. Physical Body, are you now willing to dialogue with me at this time?

I break into loud sobs and do EFT to calm myself. Then I hear the following:

PHYSICAL BODY. I didn't know I had a voice. Yes, I am willing to talk.

EMILY. Thank you all. I know this is unusual, but we need to be together more, and we need some forgiveness. Mental Body, are you willing to talk first, as you are the most verbal?

MENTAL BODY. I would be glad to go first. I have been under huge stress throughout this entire lifetime. It has been quite a ride, and we still have many years to go.

EMILY. Are you willing to ask for forgiveness from Physical Body?

MENTAL BODY. Well, yes, but I need to say something first.

EMILY. Please proceed.

MENTAL BODY. I just want all of you to know that I too have been under an enormous amount of pressure to always do things right.

EMILY. I realize that, and we are taking steps to help you. Thank you for your input. Now are you ready and willing to ask Physical Body for forgiveness?

Tears flow.

EMILY. It's not easy, is it, Mental Body?

MENTAL BODY. No, it is not. I feel like I have been a victim too, and I want to be noticed also.

EMILY. True, but I don't think you have been a victim of the emotional and physical parts of me.

MENTAL BODY. I get what you mean. Dear Physical Body, would you please forgive me for all the pressure I put on you for all these years? I am sorry to have done this to you. Please forgive me.

Tears flow.

PHYSICAL BODY. Thank you for asking.

More tears flow.

PHYSICAL BODY. Yes, I forgive you.

MENTAL BODY. Thank you. I love you.

PHYSICAL BODY. I love you too.

EMILY. Thank you, both of you. Now, Emotional Body, are you willing to ask Physical Body for forgiveness, and do you want to say anything first?

EMOTIONAL BODY. Yes, I had the benefit of hearing the above process, and I too have an issue. I was repressed for many of our years. I was under a great deal of distress. I realize this put huge pressure on Physical Body. Would you please forgive me, dear Physical Body?

Tears flow.

PHYSICAL BODY. Yes, I forgive you, and I thank you for asking.

EMOTIONAL BODY. I love you.

PHYSICAL BODY. I love you too.

EMILY. Thank you, my physical, mental, and emotional bodies.

I then do the self-forgiveness process from *Unconditional Forgiveness*. I feel calm and nurtured at the close of this deep connection with myself.

The forgiveness process feels so beneficial that I spend the next day doing deep forgiveness work on as many things as time allows. I include everything I still feel uncomfortable with: other people, situations, and even myself. Again, this is liberating.

Each day, I need a break from this intense inner work. I bundle up in warm clothes and walk the nature trail. Being in nature is nurturing for me on many levels. At one point on a walk, I hear the following message from my higher self:

HIGHER SELF. My dear, you are precious. Do not ever think you need to do everything perfectly. Remember, you are perfect the way you are, and you are here now to have a learning experience. If you already knew this, it would not be a learning experience.

You are doing very well. I love you. We all love you. Please lighten up on yourself, and please stop to feel our love.

As I close my retreat at Silver Falls, I marvel at all that has transpired each day. Something amazing is going on inside me.

January 22, 2013

Intrigued by the beneficial things I am learning, I begin my dialogues. I get a yes from Flexible and realize we have rarely dialogued.

EMILY. I now open a dialogue with Flexible. I still see you as a slender figure dressed in black-and-yellow stripes. Do you have anything to share with me?

FLEXIBLE. I have not really joined the team, and I would like to join at this time.

EMILY. I am so pleased!

Part of my medical treatment included a medication that caused stiffness in several parts of my body. The word *flexible* is still difficult for me to hear.

EMILY. I did not feel I could ever be flexible as long as I was taking the medication, but I took my last pill three weeks ago.

FLEXIBLE. I am aware of that. You are finished with the medication and your commitment to traditional Western medicine. It is now time to embrace some flexibility in your physical body as well as your mental body.

EMILY. Yes, it is time. I find it interesting that I dialogued with my physical, mental, and emotional bodies about a week ago. We did some wonderful forgiveness work together. Do you have more comments?

FLEXIBLE. Yes, that forgiveness process was the beginning of a new relationship between you and your body. This includes those three parts as well as a spiritual body, which also needs forgiveness and integration.

EMILY. Thank you for that important comment, and welcome to the team, Flexible. I am thrilled to have you join at last!

FLEXIBLE. I am honored, and I accept with delight.

EMILY. I now open a dialogue with Beloved. I am curious to learn what you have to share.

BELOVED. Oh, we so love you, Emily. We just want to say that we are all pleased with the dialogue work you are doing. It is now time to begin to actually acknowledge that what you are doing is not a parlor trick but profound work that needs to be continued and shared with others. You have already started to do this with your friends, and it has helped them. You eventually may share this with many others. We see you did not like the wording we used, *will share*, and wrote down *may share* instead. We understand, but we encourage you to keep sharing your work with others, as this will give you positive feedback, strength, and encouragement. Now you are ready to dialogue with another aspect. Do you see that there is no end to those who wish to dialogue with you? It is because there are few people willing to do what you are doing. Your writing is unique and a wonderful way to connect with the unseen world. Please continue.

EMILY. Yes, I will. I never know what will happen.

BELOVED. Yes! Isn't that the joy and delight of it all? Surprise! Here we are! All these amazing aspects of the whole you. Play with this idea. Enjoy it. Roll around in it as your dog would. Let your body move, relax, and savor life. Oh, you are so tightly wound, dear Emily. There. Relax the shoulders, and smile.

EMILY. Thank you. I need you all to keep reminding me to enjoy life. Please help me get out of my stuck patterns.

BELOVED. We are doing all we can. You have free will, you know. And the folk dancing on Saturday was wonderful once you stopped trying to do it perfectly. Was it not?

EMILY. Yes, it was grand fun.

January 23, 2013

In my dream last night, Creative came to visit. I get a yes that Creative is one of my aspects, and I add Creative to my dialogue list. Later in the dream, Playful came to visit. I am grateful for the reminder to be playful, which does not come easily for me.

January 25, 2013

Today I had an opportunity to practice saying no to someone. I am glad I was able to do this, and I am grateful for the person who made this situation possible. I am growing and changing.

February 11, 2013

During a phone session with energy dowser and healer Michael Hoefler, I learn that my own soul wishes to dialogue with me.

February 19, 2013

Curious to learn what this part of me might have to say, I attempt a dialogue after connecting with my support team.

EMILY. I am now ready and willing to dialogue with my own soul. Are you willing to dialogue with me?

MY SOUL. Of course I am ready and willing to dialogue with you, my dear one. I have been ready for a long time. I am thankful you have taken up this suggestion.

EMILY. Thank you. I have been told you have two things to say to me, but I would like to get to know you as well. It seems odd to be talking with my own soul in this formal manner.

MY SOUL. That is the only way you can be sure it is me who is doing the talking—for now at least. I don't have much to say about who I am. I am a high aspect of who you are. I am here only to help you on your life path, to guide and love you. I can give you additional wisdom as needed. You have been open and receptive lately. This is such an improvement. This will grow as you continue to grow. I sense some apprehension on your part, but there is never anything to fear from me. I will always be straightforward and honest with you. I am for your highest and best.

EMILY. Thank you for those words. I think I am—well, almost—ready to hear the two things you want to tell me. No, wait. I'm not ready. I am frightened, and my heart is pounding.

I breathe deeply to calm myself, and with determination, I proceed.

EMILY. Michael Hoefler says you need to say this to me directly. Please continue.

MY SOUL. He wanted us to make our own connection. We can do this anytime. We do not want to always have to wait for a place on his busy schedule to be able to communicate. I want to talk to you about your mothering. My, you are a marvelous mother, and you have given your all to your two daughters. Now it is time to give some of that incredible love to yourself. You were not expecting me to say that, were you?

EMILY. That is true, and I thought I had been loving myself lately.

MY SOUL. You are making a start, but you don't really even know how. Deep inside, you know exactly how, and this will come as you open up to who you really are. I love these precious dialogues, but more than that, I love your attempts to focus on yourself and send and feel love inside your body. That is why you choose to be in a body at this time. The energy on the earth is supportive of this work. You have not loved your body for many lifetimes. That is why it seems so strange to you, but you can learn and reexperience this. We all have love deep inside, as this is who we are. See how you love your daughters. You need to direct the same huge love you give to them at yourself. See how easy it is to talk to me?

EMILY. Yes, I was just noticing. I was afraid of a lecture about all my faults. Instead, I like the direct, gentle way you are sharing with me.

MY SOUL. I don't want to frighten you away. This communication is much too important for that to happen. I am gentle and perceptive just like you are. I am glad you made this connection today. Please continue these dialogues.

February 22, 2013

I get a yes to dialogue with Acceptance. I call in my support team, and as I reread my last two dialogues with this aspect, I see things were a bit rough. I don't see how I can accept my life without trying to change it. Acceptance feels like giving up to me.

Suddenly, I have an insight that the key is a different way of framing acceptance, but I don't know what this could be. I reread Georgie's comment of August 30, 2012 (see chapter 5): "Suppose accepting yourself exactly as you are is synonymous with being peaceful, calm, and happy." I have been trying to use this affirmation to help accept myself, but it is not working. I am frustrated and confused, but I continue.

EMILY. I am now ready and willing to dialogue with Acceptance. Do you have comments for me?

ACCEPTANCE. I would love to talk to you. You are doing many fun, exciting, new, helpful things, but your underlying motivation and thoughts behind all of this are that there is something wrong with you that you need to fix. There is nothing wrong with you. You are an eternal being having an intense physical experience, and these are all growing steps on your path. If you could relax more about your health and freely flow with divine love, this whole healing process could be an exciting exploration rather than a desperate searching.

EMILY. Wow! I think I am beginning to see and feel the difference. My body sighs with relief. Is this the different way of framing acceptance that I have been looking for?

ACCEPTANCE. Yes, it is. And remember, all is well, and you are loved—always!

EMILY. Thank you so much, Acceptance, for these helpful comments.

I get a yes to dialogue with Self-Compassion. I feel wobbly about this dialogue. I see there are no previous dialogues, only that High Judge became Self-Compassion and said this aspect is like some of the others I will need to learn. With determination to explore this part of myself, I continue.

EMILY. I now boldly state that I am ready and willing to dialogue with Self-Compassion. Are you ready and willing to dialogue with me?

SELF-COMPASSION. Of course I am ready and willing to dialogue with you, Emily. You know I am always here for you. I know this is a big issue for you, but like acceptance, it will pay off in the end. Please continue.

EMILY. Do you have anything else to say to me? I am starting to feel tired.

SELF-COMPASSION. Try to feel and see me as a huge, warm blanket of love and light that you wrap around yourself. I am not the same as acceptance. I am something you do for yourself on a daily and, later, constant basis. You judge yourself without mercy, and this results in difficulty with acceptance. Seeing and feeling the indigo-violet light of your oversoul will help as well. I suggest you do this every morning and during the day. It only takes a few seconds. I see you worrying about whether to do this while still in bed or waiting until you get up. I say do it both times and often throughout the day, especially when you have to make a decision. Just relax into the arms of this holy light of who you are, and feel the comfort. You do not know how to comfort yourself, at least not in a more beneficial way. You are now in the process of learning real self-care. This starts with extreme self-compassion before you can move into self-care. Do not worry. You are right on time. This is all in divine order. I am glad you came to talk to me today. See? It is never as scary as you think it is going to be. I am moving into my new role well, which means you are doing your work. Please keep this up.

EMILY. Thank you so much, and I remember your old role was High Judge. You really did clarify things for me. I love all of my aspects!

Chart of Aspects as of February 22, 2013

New Name	Previous Name	Date First Noted	Date Fully Integrated
Tenacity	Rigid Taskmaster	4-7-12	5-8-12
Courage	Stern Enforcer	4-7-12	5-8-12
Flexible	Saboteur	6-4-12	1-22-13
Balanced	Defective	6-12-12	8-11-12
Beloved	Unlovable	6-12-12	9-10-12
Precious	Unworthy	6-12-12	11-6-12
Clarity	Overwhelmed and Confused	6-20-12	9-5-12
Conscience	Guilt	6-20-12	8-3-12
Organized	Perfectionist	7-9-12	8-13-12
Let It Be	Judge's Eye	7-13-12	7-13-12
Self-Esteem Self-Assured	Sick Hospital Patient Self-Esteem	7-25-12 10-3-12	10-3-12
Safety Team and Security Force	Safety Team and Security Force	8-3-12	8-3-12
Intuition	Super-Responsible One	8-6-12	8-6-12
Joy	Sadness	8-6-12	8-6-12
Strength	Inadequate	8-11-12	8-11-12
Acceptance	Pity	8-27-12	9-5-12

Playful	Shy One	8-27-12	8-27-12
Takes Action and Connected to Source	Fear	9-10-12	9-10-12
	Inability to Say No	9-11-12	
Integrity	Anger	9-11-12	9-11-12
	People Pleaser	9-12-12	
Adventurous	Snit and Snat	9-21-12	11-6-12
Self-Compassion	High Judge	11-19-12	11-19-12
Trust and Faith in Self	Black Woman in Dream	12-12-12	
Creative	Creative	1-23-13	1-23-13

Chapter 10

It Is Impossible
to Fail at Life

March 13, 2013

I GET A YES to dialogue with Joy.

EMILY. I am curious about what you have to say, Joy.

JOY. I am not a silly, fluffy aspect. Somehow, you have gotten the idea that you are doing your life right if you are giddy and lighthearted all the time. Then as soon as this feeling is gone—and feelings pass quickly—you feel like a failure at life. It is impossible to fail at life, but you keep feeling that way anyway. I will try to explain another way. You just heard a person playing loud, booming music outside, and you started to feel resentment and anger, yes?

EMILY. Yes, I did.

JOY. Happiness comes through forgiveness. The other day, when you were on a hike, you were able to look at the noisy people nearby in a different way. This helped to reduce your resentment. I encourage you to try this practice with the booming noise outside. I love you in joy, the inner feeling that comes with peace.

EMILY. Thank you. This is so helpful!

I now get a yes to dialogue with Self-Compassion.

SELF-COMPASSION. Please reread our last dialogue.

EMILY. I just did, and I am feeling anxious about talking with you. I always feel as if I have not lived up to someone's standards when I think of acceptance and self-compassion. Can you please help me with these issues?

SELF-COMPASSION. I will try my best. You see, your aspects, being parts of you, are growing and expanding just as you are growing and expanding. Yes, we are not perfect either. What a relief! Source is the only perfect energy, but since Source is a part of us, then we have everything we really need. We are all in the process of accepting and allowing Source to express through us. Please sit with this. This is where you let go of all judgment and allow self-acceptance and self-compassion to enter. It is all a process of self-learning, and you are doing just that. We encourage you to relax and enjoy the process more. You are a joy, and we all love you.

EMILY. Thank you so much. I love you too. I am glad you came today, as I have been forgetting to wrap myself in the blanket of love and light. It feels wonderful. And I just remembered that judging another is the same as judging myself.

I notice that aspects can speak for my whole group of aspects as well as themselves.

March 22, 2013

I had an upsetting dream last night. I was a policewoman questioning a disturbed fourteen-year-old girl who had just shot her parents. I was being gentle but firm. I knew she needed help. I would like to make some sense of this traumatic dream, so I gather my courage, step into the unknown, and ask.

EMILY. Is the disturbed fourteen-year-old girl from my dream last night ready and willing to talk to me?

DISTURBED FOURTEEN-YEAR-OLD GIRL. Yes.

EMILY. Thank you. Are you able to tell me why you came into my dream last night and what you were trying to show me?

DISTURBED FOURTEEN-YEAR-OLD GIRL. I'm upset with you for dragging your feet in regard to working on Inability to Say No and People Pleaser. You have not done People Pleaser's assignment and have only done the assignment given by Inability to Say No one or two times. I came to shake you up a bit. I am not a new aspect but a part of these two. I came to represent both of them. You have been skirting around these two areas as if they don't exist, but they are hampering your wonderful progress. Please make plans to follow through on the assignments as soon as possible. I tried to get your attention over the last few days, but it was not working, so I brought you the disturbing dream.

EMILY. I am amazed at the helpful information I get when I do this work. Thank you so much!

DISTURBED FOURTEEN-YEAR-OLD GIRL. We are all here to help you in this lifetime. Remember, we are aspects of you, and you do not need to be afraid to talk to us.

EMILY. Yes, I keep forgetting. I now open a dialogue with Inability to Say No. Do you have comments for me?

INABILITY TO SAY NO. Yes, I have comments. First of all, you have a misunderstanding of what it means to say no. You will need to start back at the two-and-a-half-year-old level, but eventually, you will get up to your current age and realize it is not just about saying no to others. It is about stopping to be aware of the situation and then making a sound decision. This morning was a good example, when you gave a strong no to a request and then went ahead and helped the other person anyway. This was not a defeat, as you seem to be feeling, but a change of mind when you saw how much the request meant to the other. Saying no is not black and white. Please honor yourself for what you did this morning.

EMILY. I never looked at it that way before. Thank you. This is giving me more incentive to try the saying-no assignments.

INABILITY TO SAY NO. You are close to understanding this area and integrating this powerful concept, the ability to constructively say no.

EMILY. Thank you. And I just heard you say another other uncomfortable word: *powerful*. I'll leave that for another time.

April 6, 2013

I call in my support team and proceed.

EMILY. I am ready and willing to dialogue with Acceptance. Do you have comments for me?

ACCEPTANCE. Oh, Emily, you are so hard on yourself. Why do you not awaken and burst into joy at another precious day in your lovely body? We see you checking and scanning for possible problems. Yes, we do see you thanking God for the new day, which is an improvement, but it is hardly bursting with joy. You have to do that for yourself. It only takes a small commitment. Please give it a try. There you go. We saw your shoulders relax. Yes, we know how committed you are to your soul growth, but we also know you can do this work in joy as well. It's about accepting yourself as an intense person but one who is willing to act on suggestions. See how this feels for you. Then move on to working on saying no. Can you reframe that as a fun thing to do instead of an obligation?

EMILY. Wait a minute. I have been afraid I will not be able to learn to say no in a constructive way. Now you tell me it might even be a fun thing to do. Please explain.

ACCEPTANCE. I think it is up to someone else to explain this.

EMILY. Thank you.

I get a yes to talk to Inability to Say No.

EMILY. Do you have comments?

INABILITY TO SAY NO. I certainly do. This is all well and fine, but you need to use your pastels right now to let out some fears before you can proceed. Remember, my requests are never as scary as you think they will be, so dive in. And the process in the expressive-painting book would be excellent for you at this time.

EMILY. Thank you. Here I go.

Again, there is no how-to book to follow. I act on the suggestions of my aspects.

I begin with a large sheet of paper and my pastels. I imagine being my two-and-a-half-year-old self and say, "No," over and over in my two-and-a-half-year-old voice as I draw the huge word *no* on the page. I fill one side and fold the page in half. I fill this half page with *no* words, shouting loudly. This leads to stomping my feet as I draw and shout, "No!" over and over. I continue until the page is too tight to fold again, and I start on another page. It is liberating.

Suddenly, a huge insight comes over me: I realize I was not allowed to say no as a two-and-a-half-year-old; I learned it was not ladylike to say no. I reel as the ramifications of this debilitating belief unfold within me. What I needed was to be heard, respected, and valued as worthy when I said no, but that did not happen to my little two-and-a-half-year-old self. The next day, I burn the pages.

April 24, 2013

I call in my support team and get a yes to dialogue with Precious.

EMILY. Do you have any comments for me, Precious?

PRECIOUS. Oh, Emily, we surround you with love. We see you trying hard to feel worthy, and we want you to know deeply that you were never unworthy. This was only a misperception. You are united with Creator. This is who you are, and there is nothing you can ever do to not be this. You are at one with every aspect of creation. It can never be otherwise. You are just now beginning to experience a wee bit of what you are, and we all rejoice. Thank you for this connection today.

EMILY. Oh, thank you so much. I love all of you, my dear, wise aspects.

May 17, 2013

Feeling the need to do some concentrated work on my issues, I take myself on a retreat to a lovely cabin in the woods at Silver Falls State Park. I call in my support team and begin the exploration.

EMILY. I am now ready and willing to open a dialogue with Intuition. Please comment.

INTUITION. Please reread our first and only conversation.

EMILY. I just did, and you have a long history of being my super-responsible part. I am now trying to shift my thinking and feeling to you as my intuition. I am having trouble with this connection. Would you please speak to this?

INTUITION. I certainly will. I feel this has kept us apart in some way. Actually, we can never be apart, as we are all aspects of you, but we can sit waiting until we are acknowledged. I think you heard the medical intuitive recently tell you that you are an ancient, wise, intuitive being, yes? Well, now is the time to start to claim this part of yourself. Feels a little scary and exciting at the same time, yes?

EMILY. It certainly does feel both scary and exciting. I have been working hard at many things, hoping to be more open to my intuition. Please continue.

INTUITION. There is that phrase: *working hard*. That is how you have been taught to do your life. That will be changing. In fact, it has already started changing. You are now noticing how much you are being supported by the universe, yes?

EMILY. Yes, I see a beginning.

INTUITION. Well, it only gets better. You have been supported all along, but due to your negative, fear-based thoughts, fear is what has been showing up in your life. Underneath all this has been—and always will be—your wise, ancient, intuitive self, and that part is beginning to awaken and shine. Yes, we are thrilled, and do not worry about the super-responsible part. We can help you and guide you to know what to do and when. Your current work (we laugh at that word) regarding Inability to Say No is most important. A suggestion is to rethink the word *work* into something else, such as *process, practice,* or *procedure*— something with less of a load.

EMILY. Thank you. Do you have more comments?

INTUITION. Not at this time. We love you and are glad you are opening up to us.

I spend most of this day doing forgiveness work for anyone and anything that comes to mind. This leads to a huge self-forgiveness process regarding my inability to say no.

Suddenly, I have an insight. Maybe this is one of the things I came here to do: release my inability to say no and learn to calmly, assertively, objectively, and compassionately say no. This sounds like a life goal. I take a big breath and say the following to my higher self:

EMILY. I don't think I can learn to say no reasonably.

HIGHER SELF. Dear Emily, you have made much progress toward this goal. You just don't see it now because you have forgotten what state you were in just six years ago. Think back on that time, and see the huge progress you have made. You really are learning to say no just the way you outlined it above. Continue to do what you are led to do toward this goal. I am proud of you.

I pull out my paper and pastels and practice saying no just as I did before. However, this time, my *no* words morph into the words and actions of an adult instead of a two-and-a-half-year-old. I burn the paper in the fire pit. It is satisfying. I feel empowered!

EMILY. I now open to a dialogue with Beloved. Do you have comments for me?

BELOVED. I am pleased at the way you are diving into the processes around your supposed inability to say no. You will be able to say no in a compassionate, calm way that is clear enough to be heard by all who need to hear. Please do not be discouraged. We in this viewpoint are all excited for you. Keep doing what you are doing.

EMILY. Thank you. I now open a dialogue with Playful.

PLAYFUL. I need to say something about the fairies, sprites, and nature elementals here at Silver Falls Park. They are lively, wonderful, and playful. I am pleased you have noticed them. Maybe they will come to you in your dreams tonight.

EMILY. I would like that very much. Good night, all.

That night, I seem to be in a partial dream state. I start to go down into my all-too-familiar place of self-pity as I remember an unpleasant high school home economics teacher who would pick on me and degrade me during class. At the time, I did not even think of speaking up for myself, and I never mentioned the situation to anyone.

However, in this dream state, I find myself being held, comforted, and coached by my higher self. I then see myself speaking up assertively with great clarity. I tell the teacher to stop speaking to me in that manner and point out how inappropriate she is being. I am not shouting. There is no need.

Then I experience the same thing with several other painful memories of times when I did not speak up for myself. This time, however, I say no with clarity, calmness, and power. I feel strong and self-assured.

Upon awakening, I know amazing things are happening inside me.

May 18, 2013

I get a yes to dialogue with Inability to Say No. I am a little apprehensive about this, so I reread our last dialogues.

EMILY. All I can say is wow!

INABILITY TO SAY NO. Now do you see how powerful this work really is? You did the pastel work over the last two days and integrated it during the night. We applaud your application of our suggestions. We are really pleased!

EMILY. Thank you. Does this mean you are ready to integrate with the team as Ability to Say No?

ABILITY TO SAY NO. Yes, it does. I am ready to integrate, and I would like a celebration too!

EMILY. I am pleased! This has been quite a project. I now welcome Ability to Say No to the team.

I sing and dance around the room with glee. Then I write an affirmation: "I now have the ability to say no in a clear, compassionate way with love for all involved."

EMILY. I now open a dialogue with Trust and Faith in Self. I see you have not integrated. Please comment.

TRUST AND FAITH IN SELF. I sense you are a bit uncomfortable with talking to me.

EMILY. Yes, I am. I will reread our last dialogue of December 12, 2012. That was an extremely stressful time for me, and I am just beginning the assignment you gave me. Please continue.

TRUST AND FAITH IN SELF. Do you see what you just did? You just felt a little off and checked for the presence of uninvited influences in your energy field. Now you can take steps to clear them. This is great!

I proceed with the steps given in the book *Unified* by Roger Lanphear. I use his process to clear uninvited influences, and then I feel much better.

TRUST AND FAITH IN SELF. You always know more than you think. Knowing is not the same as thinking.

EMILY. Are you referring to my knowing that my aspects are real rather than thinking about them as being real?

My logical mind tells me that what I am doing is highly doubtful, yet I see and feel what is happening. It is real indeed.

TRUST AND FAITH IN SELF. We are real, and the more you work and play with us, the more you will realize how real we are. It is great fun!

EMILY. Yes, it is. I am amazed every time I hold a dialogue. I do not feel you are ready to integrate now. Is that true?

TRUST AND FAITH IN SELF. It is not I who is not ready to integrate; it is you who needs to be ready for me to integrate. When you are more comfortable, we will talk about full integration, but that is not as far away as you think. I love you.

EMILY. I love you too.

July 2, 2013

I meet with Georgie, and we discuss her recent idea of holding an inner-team workshop. Georgie says this material needs to be shared and will benefit others. Some part of me knows this to be true as well. Georgie will facilitate, and I will share my dialogue process and some of my dialogues. Then we will invite participants to identify and dialogue with their own aspects.

Usually, I would be terrified of such an event; however, I have recently had a series of dreams in which I am seated on a small platform with Georgie, sharing my dialogues in front of a group of people. During the past few years, I have come to trust that my dreams have wisdom for me, so I am at least open to a discussion about a workshop.

July 6, 2013

I get a yes to dialogue with My Soul.

EMILY. I am guessing you would always be open and willing to talk to me.

I burst out in nervous laughter. I don't know why I am so anxious about talking to my own soul, but I am. I listen quietly.

MY SOUL. Emily, Emily, Emily. You are a delight. You have no idea how much joy you bring to others. In fact, you are just beginning to open yourself to your own joy. Yes, it is bubbling over from deep inside of you most wonderfully. I see you are apprehensive about talking to me. Well, that will not always be so. We have much to share, you and I. It would be helpful for you to open these dialogues with me more frequently—but all in good time.

EMILY. Thank you so much. I feel better now. Please comment on Georgie's idea of an inner-team workshop.

MY SOUL. Oh, it is delightful. As you would say in your modern language, go for it! Yes, I totally approve. It will be a great success and will be of help to many others. And please don't sit and dialogue this entire day, as it is gorgeous outside.

July 13, 2013

I connect with my support team and begin.

EMILY. I am now ready and willing to dialogue with My Soul regarding an inner-team workshop. Georgie has set the date for September 14, 2013. Are you open to dialogue?

MY SOUL. Of course. You do not need to be this formal. You can talk to me at any time, but I appreciate your preparation. This makes for a clear message. I think the workshop with Georgie will be marvelous for you and for others. Remember, you are a conduit for this work. You are setting an example. Each participant can do the process his or her own way, and that will be good. Relax, and enjoy the preparations. You do not need to do the work yourself. Let the universe run the show. You just show up and share your part. That is a good date, by the way. Do not put it off until November, when the energy will be more of a pensive winter mode. That energy can be good, depending on what you want to do, but September is the best time to teach others new things. I love you.

EMILY. Thank you. I love you too.

July 22, 2013

I connect with my support team.

I recently had a session with Jean Haner, a practitioner in the Chinese art of reading facial features. She said I intuitively knew the needs of others and would naturally take steps to help them. My astrology chart said basically the same thing. Both said I could easily do this at my own expense.

EMILY. I am now ready and willing to dialogue with People Pleaser. Do you have comments for me?

PEOPLE PLEASER. I see you do not have our other conversations with you today, but we will proceed from here anyway. It would have been helpful, but maybe that is just as well. One of the things I said was that you will find it difficult and strange not to have me in my usual role.

EMILY. Thank you. I have been working on asserting my own self and my truths and not trying to always be liked by others.

PEOPLE PLEASER. True, but remember what the expert in Chinese face reading said about you being the perfect hostess who knows how to meet everyone's needs.

EMILY. I do, but I also know that I do not have to do that at the expense of my own needs.

PEOPLE PLEASER. We will see how this goes. I am glad you are at least saying the words. This is a huge life lesson you came to learn. Why else would you have chosen the face and body you did, as well as the astrological chart you did? Yes, it is time to take on this one, so to speak.

EMILY. Thank you for the comments. Do you have any more?

PEOPLE PLEASER. Well, let me see. I think I will stop here.

EMILY. Do you have another more positive title for me to use?

PEOPLE PLEASER. Try some out for me, will you?

EMILY. No, that is your job. What are some possibilities?

PEOPLE PLEASER. I see you are going to make me do the work. Okay, here goes. How about the name Likeable, Good-Natured, In Tune with Others, Guided, or Connected to Others?

EMILY. That is a marvelous list! I am amazed. Do you think you will be able to choose one and integrate before the September 14 workshop?

PEOPLE PLEASER. Whew! I was afraid I had to choose and integrate today. I am not ready for that, but I am sure I will be ready by September 13, in the morning.

EMILY. Could you please make that September 10 to give some leeway?

PEOPLE PLEASER. I am sure that could be arranged.

EMILY. Thank you so much, and thank you for the dialogue today.

PEOPLE PLEASER. You are most welcome. Goodbye for now.

I do not feel that I am finished with this dialogue, so I stop and go through a decision-making process regarding a new title for this aspect. I come up with Guided as the top choice and In Tune with Others as my second choice.

EMILY. People Pleaser, are you willing to sit with the title of Guided or In Tune with Others?

PEOPLE PLEASER. There you go again, trying to be so people pleasing. The title Guided came up with the highest scores, so just do it. Yes, I like Guided very much.

EMILY. So do I. Can we make this your new title?

PEOPLE PLEASER. Yes. Finally got that job done! I thought this would never happen.

EMILY. I am practicing being guided.

I smile.

PEOPLE PLEASER. Very funny. Actually, that was a good one. And I think I might be ready to integrate too.

EMILY. Marvelous! I have been wondering if this moment would ever come. I am pleased! I now officially welcome Guided to the team.

GUIDED. This is more of an honor than I thought it would be. I am pleased to be on the team. I know you still have a lot to learn, but I am here for you and with you.

EMILY. Thank you so much!

I light a candle in honor of the integration of Guided to the team.

Chart of Aspects as of July 22, 2013

New Name	Previous Name	Date First Noted	Date Fully Integrated
Tenacity	Rigid Taskmaster	4-7-12	5-8-12
Courage	Stern Enforcer	4-7-12	5-8-12
Flexible	Saboteur	6-4-12	1-22-13
Balanced	Defective	6-12-12	8-11-12
Beloved	Unlovable	6-12-12	9-10-12
Precious	Unworthy	6-12-12	11-6-12
Clarity	Overwhelmed and Confused	6-20-12	9-5-12
Conscience	Guilt	6-20-12	8-3-12
Organized	Perfectionist	7-9-12	8-13-12
Let It Be	Judge's Eye	7-13-12	7-13-12
Self-Assured	Sick Hospital Patient Self-Esteem	7-25-12 10-3-12	10-3-12
Safety Team and Security Force	Safety Team and Security Force	8-3-12	8-3-12
Intuition	Super-Responsible One	8-6-12	8-6-12
Joy	Sadness	8-6-12	8-6-12
Strength	Inadequate	8-11-12	8-11-12
Acceptance	Pity	8-27-12	9-5-12

Playful	Shy One	8-27-12	8-27-12
Takes Action and Connected to Source	Fear	9-10-12	9-10-12
Ability to Say No	Inability to Say No	9-11-12	5-18-13
Integrity	Anger	9-11-12	9-11-12
Guided	People Pleaser	9-12-12	7-22-13
Adventurous	Snit and Snat	9-21-12	11-6-12
Self-Compassion	High Judge	11-19-12	11-19-12
Trust and Faith in Self	Black Woman in Dream	12-12-12	
Creative	Creative	1-23-13	1-23-13

Chapter 11

You Are Always Safe

September 3, 2013

I CALL IN MY support team and ask each aspect if she is willing to be a part of the Inner-Team workshop. I feel the energy of each one. Some are bursting to share, some are not so enthusiastic but willing, and a few decline to participate.

September 13, 2013

I get a yes from Acceptance, and I reread our last dialogue. I feel like such a failure when it comes to everything Acceptance said. Even though I know all those wonderful words are true, I still feel I have so much to fix, and I am certainly not in the free-flow part at all. I am tired and take a short nap.

I do not see how I will learn, grow, and expand if I accept myself, and what is the need for expansion anyway? I am determined, however, to learn from this intriguing aspect of mine, so I continue.

EMILY. I am ready and willing to dialogue with Acceptance. Please comment.

ACCEPTANCE. You will be expanding differently. You will be coming from a solid base of accepting yourself rather than from a wobbly sense of someone who needs to be fixed. There is a huge difference in the energy of these two states. Think about it, and feel the difference.

EMILY. Thank you. I will do that.

I am in the garage studio, and a friendly cat strolls in to visit me. I laugh. The little visitor is helping me to lighten up a bit.

EMILY. I think I have much work to do in order to accept myself. My inner self has been miserable for so much of my life. Please comment.

ACCEPTANCE. Yes, I will comment. If you had nothing to accept about yourself, there would be no point in acceptance. You chose this path because you wanted to learn this valuable life lesson and then be able to expand from a solid base of total acceptance. We all hope you begin a process of self-acceptance soon. It will be a huge relief when you have done even some of this work, and it will help your family and friends as well. I leave you in love.

September 14, 2013

Georgie and I offer the Inner-Team workshop, and many people attend. Georgie facilitates the process, and I share some of my dialogues. We invite everyone present to identify one of his or her own aspects and then dialogue with the aspect. Every person is able to participate. It is exciting and amazing!

I am especially excited because until this day, I was unsure others had aspects. Not only does each person have aspects, but they are all able to dialogue with at least one part of themselves. It is extremely rewarding.

October 14, 2013

I am now in a new location, and I am sharing a small heated apartment with a friend. I have the space every Monday beginning in December. As I begin my dialogue with Beloved, I wonder if any of this is real.

EMILY. Do you have comments for me, Beloved?

BELOVED. Oh my, yes, this is real! Please do not ever doubt. Many in the unseen world care so much about you, dear Emily, and wish to see you continue your dialogues. You do not yet realize the importance of these dialogues. You are one of only a few people doing what you are now doing. Please do not ever doubt. There is so much help for you here. We encourage you to continue.

EMILY. Thank you so much, Beloved, for your kind, strong words of encouragement.

November 4, 2013

I am currently working through the book *Unified* by Roger Lanphear and doing every process as suggested.

I get a yes to dialogue with Courage. I start to go into fear. Why would I be needing courage? Was something bad going to happen?

EMILY. I am now ready and willing, although a little apprehensive, to dialogue with Courage.

COURAGE. I am smiling that you are apprehensive. Do you still doubt you are a courageous woman? If so, even a tiny bit, please let that go. You are an extremely courageous person. Not many people have the courage to want to get to know who they really are. Your work with the *Unified* book is helping, as is all of this. Please continue. This is exciting work. Actually, it is play work, as it is exciting, fun, and joyous. We are pleased!

EMILY. Thank you. I love knowing you are on the team. I now open a dialogue with Precious. Please comment.

PRECIOUS. We love these conversations! Yes, you are courageous. We know you had a bit of unworthiness come up yesterday. That is all right, as this energy is currently moving out of your system. Someday soon, you will not even be able to remember what being unworthy felt like. You will just know deeply that you are a child of God, and there will be no doubt whatsoever. Love and blessings to you! We are complete.

EMILY. Thank you so much. I now open a dialogue with Acceptance. Do you have comments?

ACCEPTANCE. Please reread our last dialogues and the comments by Georgie on self-acceptance. See how far you have come, dear Emily. This is another reason it is important to read and reread your dialogues. They carry profound information. You will someday be led to share this with many others but not yet. You are in a powerful process of self-growth. If you could see yourself energetically, you would be surprised. Your light and energy are glowing much more brightly. Just wrap self-acceptance around that. This is already leading to more acceptance of others. We are all here to help each other. Blessings on this day.

November 5, 2013

During our session today, Georgie says I will know when I have fully accepted myself because I will be at peace. I look forward to that day.

November 11, 2013

I have long been wanting to put safety on my list of aspects, but I have never had a dialogue with Safe. Today I get a yes to dialogue with Safe.

EMILY. Please comment.

SAFE. I am not really an aspect and wish to be removed from consideration as an aspect. Now that you are learning more about who you really are, I think you will agree that you are always safe, as you cannot be otherwise. You are a child of God, and you are an eternal being. What could be safer? This is all part of your growth experience. Be well. Of course, you cannot be otherwise.

I hear laughter.

EMILY. Amazing! I now open a dialogue with Tenacity. Please comment.

TENACITY. Just like Courage, I have never really dialogued with you, and I would like to be included.

EMILY. I am ready for your comments. Please continue.

TENACITY. Oh, Emily, you are the most tenacious of women; in fact, you amaze even me. Now I think it is time to relax and think more about going with the flow. You didn't think you would hear that from me, did you? Well, surprise!

EMILY. I could not imagine what you were going to say. Thank you so much, Tenacity. A book about living in the flow just popped into my awareness the other day. Do you have more comments?

TENACITY. No, I am sure you will be tenacious about learning to live in the flow also. We all love you. Good evening.

Georgie said there would come a time when I'd identified and integrated all of my aspects. I am a little sad about this thought, as I am really enjoying discovering each of them, but I also wish to have the experience of being whole. My aspects tell me this will happen when I have integrated with all of them. In the meantime, I see that I have not integrated with Trust and Faith in Self, and I anxiously reread my only two dialogues with this aspect.

EMILY. I boldly state that I am ready and willing to dialogue with Trust and Faith in Self.

A slight pain passes quickly through my head as I write this, and I check for uninvited influences. I get a no that there are none, so I continue.

EMILY. Are you ready and willing to dialogue with me?

TRUST AND FAITH IN SELF. Yes, I am willing to dialogue with you, Emily. I have a few things to say. I am glad you reread our two conversations and now know the background. You do not have sufficient trust in yourself and, therefore, faith in yourself to warrant integration at this time. Maybe after you attend the Sonia Choquette workshop in a few days, this will change. Please connect with us again soon.

EMILY. Thank you for your honesty.

I think this lack of trust is the reason for the head pain, and I feel led to look up *trust* and *faith* in my dictionary. *Trust* is defined as firm belief in the reliability, truth, or strength of a person or thing, or confident expectation. *Faith* is defined as reliance, trust, or belief in religious doctrine; loyalty; or sincerity.

I certainly do not feel confident expectation or any of the other nice words as I do these dialogues. However, I am curious and determined to be as whole as possible, so I continue.

I recently had a strong urge to sign up for Sonia Choquette's Trust Your Vibes, Level 1 workshop. Despite the fact that I feel inadequate to go, I sign up anyway. Who knows what I might discover?

November 15–17, 2013

I attend Sonia's Trust Your Vibes, Level 1 workshop. It is amazing, and I surprise myself by being able to participate.

December 2, 2013

Back at the studio, I get a yes to dialogue with Flexible.

EMILY. I am curious to hear from you, Flexible. Please comment.

FLEXIBLE. I loved the dancing and moving at the Trust Your Vibes workshop. Can we please do more of that?

EMILY. I would like to. Thank you for the prompt. I now open a dialogue with Fear. Please comment.

I am apprehensive, as I had an encounter with a person this morning in which I became fearful.

FEAR. I really came up for you this morning during your interaction with that person. I am pleased you realized you were being driven by your fear, even if you were not able to do anything about it at the time. At least you recognized it.

EMILY. Thank you. I do not feel safe with that person. I don't know if I ever will.

FEAR. That is not what one who is made in the image of God would say.

EMILY. Yes, that is true. I don't understand how you could have integrated as Takes Action and Connected to Source but show up as Fear.

FEAR. Just because we integrate does not mean we will never show up as our first title. Remember, fear is not a bad thing. It is a basic self-protection. Fear will be with you as long as you feel you need protecting. You are close to a time when you will be able to release all fear of that person. Power has something to do with this. Please ask if power is an aspect you have been avoiding, even if subconsciously.

EMILY. Thank you.

I ask if I have an aspect called Powerful, and I get a yes. I am not sure if I like where this is going, but the words *power* and *powerful* have been flitting through my mind all afternoon, and I even jotted them down on a scrap of paper.

EMILY. I am now ready and willing to open a dialogue with Powerful. Do you have anything to say to me at this time?

POWERFUL. Oh my, yes, I do. I have been waiting a long time for this to happen. You have no idea how long. It has been more than this lifetime. You have not felt powerful for a few lifetimes, but that is about to change. Your work with the *Unified* material has tipped the scales, so to speak, and you are now ready. The forgiveness work was the beginning, and the momentum has been building since then. Please do not be afraid, for you are being led and guided all the way. This is only happening as you are ready. Being powerful does not mean shouting back at others. No. It is quite different. It means fully knowing who you are and coming from a deep place of confidence and knowledge. Each day, you are learning more about who you really are. It is exciting, is it not?

EMILY. I hardly know what to say. Thank you for nudging me to open this dialogue. I am just trying to listen and put one foot ahead of the other. Again, thank you. Do you have any more for me?

POWERFUL. Not at this time.

EMILY. Are you fully integrated?

POWERFUL. Not yet. Let's give this some time, but this is my final title.

EMILY. Thank you again. I am in awe!

POWERFUL. This will change when you accept me. I love you.

EMILY. I love you too.

Chart of Aspects as of December 2, 2013

New Name	Previous Name	Date First Noted	Date Fully Integrated
Tenacity	Rigid Taskmaster	4-7-12	5-8-12
Courage	Stern Enforcer	4-7-12	5-8-12
Flexible	Saboteur	6-4-12	1-22-13
Balanced	Defective	6-12-12	8-11-12
Beloved	Unlovable	6-12-12	9-10-12
Precious	Unworthy	6-12-12	11-6-12
Clarity	Overwhelmed and Confused	6-20-12	9-5-12
Conscience	Guilt	6-20-12	8-3-12
Organized	Perfectionist	7-9-12	8-13-12
Let It Be	Judge's Eye	7-13-12	7-13-12
Self-Assured	Sick Hospital Patient Self-Esteem	7-25-12 10-3-12	10-3-12
Safety Team and Security Force	Safety Team and Security Force	8-3-12	8-3-12
Intuition	Super-Responsible One	8-6-12	8-6-12
Joy	Sadness	8-6-12	8-6-12
Strength	Inadequate	8-11-12	8-11-12
Acceptance	Pity	8-27-12	9-5-12

Playful	Shy One	8-27-12	8-27-12
Takes Action and Connected to Source	Fear	9-10-12	9-10-12
Ability to Say No	Inability to Say No	9-11-12	5-18-13
Integrity	Anger	9-11-12	9-11-12
Guided	People Pleaser	9-12-12	7-22-13
Adventurous	Snit and Snat	9-21-12	11-6-12
Self-Compassion	High Judge	11-19-12	11-19-12
Trust and Faith in Self	Black Woman in Dream	12-12-12	
Creative	Creative	1-23-13	1-23-13
Powerful	Powerful	12-2-13	

Chapter 12

You Are Never Alone

December 9, 2013

TODAY I ENJOY THE new apartment space for my work and marvel at the synchronicity of how it all happened at the right time. I explore the seven chakras and have time for a dialogue with Precious.

PRECIOUS. My former title was Unworthy, and I feel now that you are almost 100 percent in acceptance of the idea that you are indeed worthy of God's love. Are you not?

EMILY. Yes, you are correct. I did not even give it much thought when I began the *Unified* lesson in which we were to feel God's love. I had doubts I could feel that love, but I did not have doubts I deserved to feel God's love. Thank you for pointing that out to me. I love you.

December 16, 2013

Today I do exercises from the book *Tune In* by Sonia Choquette. One activity is to write, without thinking, what your heart would love to do. I find myself writing, "Fall in love with myself!" This is a surprise. I feel uncomfortable and check it out. I get a yes that I have mental blocks to loving myself, and I get a yes to dialogue with Beloved.

EMILY. I am now ready and willing to dialogue with Beloved—well, almost. I have just learned I have mental blocks to loving myself.

I take a big breath. I am now ready to proceed.

EMILY. Do you have comments for me, Beloved?

BELOVED. My, you are loved, Emily. This is all part of divine order. First, you learn and feel and get to trust that God loves you, and then you get to do the same with loving yourself. Please continue with the *Unified* process. We are smiling with joy.

EMILY. Thank you so much. I now open a dialogue with Trust and Faith in Self. Do you have comments for me?

TRUST AND FAITH IN SELF. Please reread previous dialogues. I feel you doubting your guidance. As you clear more and more of your blockages in your energy field and your cells, your guidance will be more and more accurate. This is not to say that it is not accurate and useful now. It is all just right where you need to be, so stop doubting, and trust.

EMILY. I feel my lower lip quivering and feel as if I am ready to cry. I do not feel I will ever live up to your expectations.

TRUST AND FAITH IN SELF. I have no expectations. I only mirror where you are at a given moment. I am only here to help you. There. I saw your shoulders relax. There is nothing you have to do or be at this time.

EMILY. But then you will not integrate, and I want to feel whole.

TRUST AND FAITH IN SELF. Well, that is true, but remember, it is not I who decides when we integrate. It is you who decides. You are in charge of this entire process. You do not please us; you please yourself.

EMILY. I don't understand. You mean my quivering lip is about me being disappointed in myself?

TRUST AND FAITH IN SELF. No. It is about you not knowing who and what you are. If you really knew that, you would have no doubts. The *Unified* book is good for you at this time. Please continue with the exercises.

EMILY. I will. Thank you again.

According to the book *Unified* by Roger Lanphear, we all have a higher self who has never lost its connection to God, and we have never lost the connection to our higher self. We only thought we did.

December 30, 2013

Today I work on clearing blockages from my cells. A huge sadness comes up for me as I focus on my right chest region. In May 2007, I had a right mastectomy, followed by right breast reconstruction in 2009. Many tears flow.

January 5, 2014

I participate in a burning-bowl ceremony and release many things that no longer serve me. At the close of the ceremony, I draw an angel card for the coming year, 2014. I draw the obedience angel. I am disappointed.

EMILY. I now open a dialogue with Beloved.

BELOVED. My dear Emily, we all want to assure you that there is a God, and this God cares deeply for you. We know you are just beginning to awaken to a connection with God, and we wish with all our love to see you continue with this holy process. It is very holy, and you are poised to do this now. This is the right and perfect time in your life. Someday soon, you will laugh at these doubts and wonder how you could ever have had them. Do not be afraid, for you are never alone, and there is always help and guidance available for the asking. You have gifts that will help both yourself and others, and now you are beginning to hone these gifts. Your guidance from God will tell you what to do and when, what to say and how, and whom to say it to. Yes, not everyone will be interested. That is fine. They will have another time, but many will be interested and wish to hear. This is all. We love you so.

EMILY. Thank you so much. I will ponder these words. I now open a dialogue with Self-Compassion. Please comment.

SELF-COMPASSION. We want you to reread our dialogues for several reasons. First, you will see how far you have come. You only acknowledged us a little more than a year ago. Second, they will reinforce our message. We note that you have forgotten the warm blanket of love and self-compassion we mentioned, and we think it would be helpful now. We see you connecting obedience with High Judge, but in reality, the obedience angel is merciful and will help you complete what you set out to do. In fact, she will help you complete projects with grace and ease. This all has to do with the energy you have when you begin a project. Is the energy "I must get this done now, or something bad will happen," or is it "I will call on the help of an appropriate angel, a spiritual figure, or my higher self for some help"? You do not have to do life alone. Asking for help is wise, and it is also self-compassion. There is no need to do life by yourself. There is much help for you here. We are through for today. We love you so much.

EMILY. Thank you so much. I love you too.

January 6, 2014

I am feeling anxious about the words of Self-Compassion, and I get a yes that I am blocking my higher self from benefiting me. I decide to at least ask for help and see what happens. I sit quietly and ask my support team to please help me release these blocks. I experience slight head, throat, and chest tension and do EFT tapping. Finally, I feel much better and get a no that there is nothing left to release regarding blocking help from my higher self. I can't prove this is real, but I feel much better now that the process is complete.

January 12, 2014

I have a dream I call Orphan Girl, in which I am at a community college and see children having birthday parties in my former classrooms. Then I find children who actually live there. One little girl is particularly uncared for. She doesn't have anyone helping her, so I help her get ready for bed. I find a mattress, blanket, and cuddle toy. I make a decision to take her away and find a good home for her. Then I am in a room with several odd people. One man has glued colored stones to his face for decoration, and one woman is frumpy and disheveled. I hug her and love her. She is happy with this, as no one else notices her. I realize they all need love.

January 13, 2014

I decide to try a dialogue with Little Orphan Girl from my dream noted above. I do not feel comfortable with this, but I proceed anyway.

EMILY. Do you have anything to say to me, Little Orphan Girl?

I hear nothing.

I use a process from Roger Lanphear's *Unified* to clear uninvited influences, but I still hear nothing. Frustrated at the lack of response and concerned, as I feel this little orphan girl really needs help, I make a note to try for another dialogue with her soon.

I get a yes to dialogue with Trust and Faith in Self. I reread our last two conversations and note that I always feel weak when I get a yes that this aspect wishes to dialogue.

EMILY. I now open to dialogue with Trust and Faith in Self.

TRUST AND FAITH IN SELF. Dear Emily, you do not see the enormous strides you are making. Someday you will trust yourself and have complete faith in yourself and your abilities. This means also that you will trust your guidance. You are coming steadily to trust your guidance, but somehow, you are disconnecting this as the real you. The real you is just like the *Unified* book says you are. You just need more experience before you can have trust and faith in yourself. Do not worry. It will come. And do not worry about integration. It will all happen in divine time.

January 19–22, 2014

Longing for some extended time to dive deeply into what is happening in my life, I take myself on a retreat to a heated cabin at Silver Falls State Park. For some time now, I have felt incomplete with my inner-child work. I have never been able to feel the integration of all my inner-child stages, as described by John Bradshaw in his book *Homecoming*. Determined to complete this process, I continue today in an attempt to integrate and feel the love of my inner children.

After my success on January 6, 2014, in asking my support team to release blocks to my ability to receive help from my higher self, I decide to try this approach today. I have five photos of my younger self at various ages, which I have been using to represent the stages of my inner children.

I begin with Baby Emily. I hold her photo and bravely ask my support team to please help me release my blocks to loving her and integrating with her. It is a tearful evening as I allow the blocks to release. I hug and love the photo and my own imaginary baby self. Eventually, I come to peace and know the process is complete.

The next day, I connect with my support team and ask their help to release blocks to loving my other inner children. I ask for help to release blocks to loving Toddler Emily. I send love to my toddler self and hold a photo of myself as a toddler. Again, it is a tearful experience, but it seems to work. First, I ask for the release. Then I allow energy to move inside my body and tears to flow. Finally, I feel much better.

I move to releasing blocks to loving Preschool Emily and have an insight that she had no one to go to for appreciation and acceptance of her sensitive self. I send Preschool Emily love and acceptance.

Then I ask for and receive release of blocks to loving School-Age Emily, who felt alone in the world. I send love and acceptance to this part of myself. This time, however, huge emotions, from anger to joy, surge through my body. It is liberating.

I cannot stop now, so I move to ask for release of blocks to loving Adolescent Emily, who was courageous despite extreme loneliness. She was different from anyone else in her small town. I send her love and admiration from my adult self.

Then I ask for and receive release of blocks to loving Young Adult Emily, who was determined to improve her confusing life. I surround her with love and appreciation from my adult self.

Finally, I surrender and let the process complete itself. With the help of my support team, I come to a place of integration, joy, and deep peace.

This process is going so well that I decide to experiment with releases of other uncomfortable areas. I ask for and receive release of my perfectionism and various health issues. I begin by connecting with my support team. Then I use a combination of two processes: the script from *Feelings Buried Alive Never Die* by Karol Truman and additional affirmations from *You Can Heal Your Life* by Louise Hay. I feel much better after each release.

On the last day of this amazing retreat, I happen to look at my inner-child photos. I feel love and joy for each one of them. In the past, I felt burdened whenever I looked at these pictures. I felt guilty for not loving them and thought I did not know how. It seems I only needed to release my blocks to loving them. At last, I feel I have merged with my beautiful inner children, as John Bradshaw suggested.

January 27, 2014

Today I get a yes that all aspects of my dream Little Orphan Girl (see January 12, 2014) wish to dialogue with me. I begin with Little Orphan Girl.

EMILY. What do you have to share with me today, Little Orphan Girl?

I hear nothing.

EMILY. Are you unable to talk?

I get a yes.

EMILY. Are you an aspect of Little Emily?

I get a yes.

EMILY. Did you get left behind when I merged with Little Emily last weekend at Silver Falls?

I get a no.

EMILY. Do you want to be held and acknowledged?

I get a yes.

EMILY. Are you a part of Little Emily that I just started to love?

I get a yes.

EMILY. Are the others in this dream aspects of Adult Emily?

I get a yes.

EMILY. Do they only need to be acknowledged and held as well?

I get a yes.

EMILY. Do they have other needs at this time?

I get a no.

I hug and hold Little Orphan Girl, Frumpy Woman, and Man with the Decorated Face. I feel them merge with me as I love them and rock them. I tell them I will be taking much better care of them now that I have cleared the blocks to loving these inner parts of myself.

January 28, 2014

I get a massage from a gifted massage therapist, Karen O'Neill, who has some words for me after I share the above events with her. She tells me I am regrowing cells that do not remember the old story, and the process takes a while. The new cells are like babies and need to be treated with love and gentleness. She says I am to be gentle with myself and tell myself a new story. When I am clear about who I am and start telling the truth to myself, I heal.

February 3, 2014

I get a yes to open a dialogue with People Pleaser, also called Guided.

EMILY. Do you have comments for me?

PEOPLE PLEASER, ALSO CALLED GUIDED. I knew this would not be an easy trait for you to transform. We are pleased to see you working through the *Unified* book, even if you don't feel comfortable with everything. Do you see that when you are in upset mode, the others around you become defensive? I like that you did not drop the People Pleaser portion of my title at this time. You have no faith in yourself at this time either. Keep working with *Unified*, and know that it will come. The more you do all of the above suggestions, the faster it will come. You are determined, and we know it can happen in this lifetime.

EMILY. Thank you so much.

February 10, 2014

I call in my support team.

EMILY. I am now ready and willing to dialogue with Trust and Faith in Self. Please comment.

TRUST AND FAITH IN SELF. We feel you are almost ready for us to integrate into the team. You are doing amazing work with the *Unified* material, and this is really helping you to trust. This is the first step to having real faith in yourself and your abilities. That is all for now. We love you.

EMILY. Thank you.

I receive another gift from my Silver Falls retreat. Today, for the first time, the idea comes to me to dialogue with my inner children. I decide to see if this is possible.

EMILY. I am now ready and willing to dialogue with my inner children. Do you have any comments?

INNER CHILDREN. Oh! We are all so excited to be connected to you, Big Emily. We love that at your last Silver Falls retreat, you released all the blocks you had to loving us. This is wonderful, and we love the way you look at our photos with love and caring instead of feelings that we are a burden to be dealt with. Oh, this is so much better. Wheee! We love that you took us out in the snow for three days in a row too. That was great!

EMILY. I am relieved to hear all you have to say. I was not sure how you would respond to me. You will have to tell me what you need. Or maybe you could prompt me when you need something, and we will discuss things. What do you have to say about that?

INNER CHILDREN. Oh, we like that. That way, we can begin to urge you to acknowledge us more. This will help you in many ways. You do not think we can be of help to you, but we really can. We are more closely connected to our higher self than you are, Big Emily. Honest. Even though we were unhappy, we were still more connected. Now you will listen to us. It will be great. And way more fun!

EMILY. Wow! I was expecting tears and sadness. Instead, I am met with love and joy. I am looking forward to our next adventure in getting to know each other. I love you all so much.

INNER CHILDREN. And we love the picture of dear Baby Emily up on the wall in a nicely oiled frame. Yes, this is a great beginning!

EMILY. Thank you. I love you all so very much!

I get a yes to use the script process from the book *Feelings Buried Alive Never Die* to release emotions around the belief "I don't trust myself." It is quite a process, but I finally come to peace and know it is complete—for today at least.

Next, I attempt to release the belief "When I am with an angry person, I need to please this person in order to be loved by him or her." I try to replace this belief with the statement "I no longer need to please others in order to be loved." This is all confusing for me, and I know my effort is only marginally successful.

February 11, 2014

Today I meet with Georgie, and we discuss the latest events in my inner-child work. She says, "Anger is a mask of fear. Release the anger first and then the fear." Then she suggests I look back over the past year and a half, step back to get the big picture of my life, and be in awe of what has happened.

I know much has happened with the discovery of my aspects and these amazing dialogues, but I am still surprised by her comment.

RELAX

Chapter 13

Life Is Marvelous
and Exciting

March 8–10, 2014

I ATTEND THE SONIA Choquette Trust Your Vibes, Level 2 workshop. One activity is a deep meditation in which we feel loved and nurtured by our own higher self. I am in tears. It is beautiful. This is my first experience with the power of love from my own higher self. It is incredible—freely given and available for the asking at all times.

March 10, 2014

I begin this day feeling nurtured from the loving meditation I experienced yesterday.

EMILY. I am ready to dialogue with my inner children. Do you have something to share?

INNER CHILDREN. We loved the dancing and the movement you did at the Sonia Choquette event. Please give us all a chance to do this more often, as often as even every day. Imagine every day basking in the love, nourishment, and support of our own higher self, which is our connection to the divine. Along with this is moving in our lovely physical body. This is one of the many reasons you came to Earth. You are doing much better at loving and mothering us, but there is much more you can do.

We delight in movement and color. Wheee, color! We are glad you feel the chakra colors pressing on you at this time. We would love for you to move and flow with the bright chakra colors. Let them do their magic in your body. Let the colors delight and heal you. Yes, colors can heal. Really, they can. All is energy, and colors are energy. Relax, and let yourself be one with the colors. Let them flow out of you and onto paper and fabric. Experiment with their vibrations, and don't wait to study it all. Just dive in, and play with the colors. Really look at each color. Really feel each color. See how they laugh; dance; and speak their own language of sparkles, joy, love, freedom, happiness, and excitement at being alive. Yes, they speak to joy at being alive and in a physical body and feeling what it feels like to be alive in a body. Colors have much to teach you. Allow them to be in your life and be a part of you. We are glad you chose to dialogue with us today. Wheee!

EMILY. I am glad you chose me too. I love you!

March 24, 2014

Using the script process from *Feelings Buried Alive Never Die*, I release the origin of the feelings that keep me from accepting myself and trusting myself, as well as the feelings that cause me to fail. This is all new and amazing. Can this really be real?

March 31, 2014

I get a yes to dialogue with People Pleaser, also called Guided.

EMILY. Do you have any comments for me?

PEOPLE PLEASER, ALSO CALLED GUIDED. I certainly do. The releasing of traumas using the *Feelings Buried Alive Never Die* book is helpful for you. Don't you feel the difference?

EMILY. Yes, I do, or was it the small nap I took?

PEOPLE PLEASER, ALSO CALLED GUIDED. Certainly not! You have cleared some significant blocks today. I want to suggest you release people-pleasing traits using this process as well.

EMILY. Thank you. That is a great idea. I wonder why I never thought of it before.

April 21, 2014

I am currently studying the book *Spirituality of the Third Millennium* by Roger Lanphear, and it is expanding my view of the unseen world. Today I do some deep forgiveness work.

EMILY. I now open a dialogue with Acceptance. Do you have comments for me?

ACCEPTANCE. Please reread our previous conversations.

EMILY. I just did, and it was most helpful. I now see progress.

ACCEPTANCE. You most certainly do see progress. Marvelous progress indeed! We all see you bravely taking action as guided by your intuition. And please do not think of the need for forgiveness as a sign of failure. There are no failures, only learning experiences. This is true for all beings. We will all eventually reintegrate with God, and then we will do something else marvelous and exciting. Yes, life is marvelous and exciting. We see you feeling this more and more. Everything you are doing these days is helping you. Do not worry that you are not doing a flashy teaching-the-world kind of activity. It is now time for you to relax, remember, and integrate all that is opening up for you. We are all pleased to be on the team. We see you beginning to accept who you really are, and that is lovely. We close for now in love and light.

May 5, 2014

At the time of my cancer diagnosis, I was led to Spring Forest Qigong, a powerful Chinese healing practice. I continue this practice daily, and it provides great support.

Last week, I attended the annual Spring Forest Qigong Conference and came away from a powerful healing session with these words in my mind: "I trust myself" and "I trust my higher self."

Yesterday I found myself saying a firm but necessary no to another person, which was new for me.

EMILY. I now open a dialogue with Ability to Say No. Do you have comments for me?

ABILITY TO SAY NO. You bet I have comments. I am excited that you are finding your voice and beginning to say no when it is needed.

EMILY. Thank you. I didn't realize what a new thing I was doing. It just happened.

I now get a yes to dialogue with Trust and Faith in Self.

EMILY. Do you have comments for me?

TRUST AND FAITH IN SELF. Dear Emily, we are extremely proud of you! Do you see the enormous strides you have made over only the last two weeks? See how easily and surely the universe lines up to support you when all is ready! You recently had three events that are pivotal to your advancement. They all seemingly just popped into place: your forgiveness work, a broadened perspective of the unseen world, and trust. This is only the beginning of another phase of a new life for yourself. We look forward to taking this trip with you, and yes, we are ready to integrate and be on the team.

EMILY. I am amazed. Thank you. I am at a loss for words.

TRUST AND FAITH IN SELF. There is no need for words. In fact, we want you to just feel. Feel how easily you are accepting this honor. You are not quivering in fear and self-doubt. No, you are just putting one word after another with sureness and ease. This is thrilling. And more than that, we want you to be grateful for your gifts and be open to trusting our communication.

EMILY. I see. First, I trust in myself, and then I will progress to trusting in my guidance.

TRUST AND FAITH IN SELF. Yes, that is the way it is. We close in love and light.

EMILY. Thank you.

I add Trust and Faith in Guidance to my list of aspects.

EMILY. I now open a dialogue with Perfectionist.

PERFECTIONIST. I wish to clarify that my new title is Organized, and I have a comment about the trusting-self healing you received at the Spring Forest Qigong event. This will change how you look at my perfectionist part. Being a perfectionist will no longer hold center stage, and being organized will take over. This will be a relief for you and will not cause any problems. I am pleased this all came about. I close in love and light as well.

EMILY. I just realized I made an error in the keying of your new title, but I made the correction easily. I am sorry I confused your titles. Is this an example of what you are talking about? I no longer need to berate myself, a lifelong habit, for each tiny error?

ORGANIZED. Yes, that is exactly what it means. Congratulations! Your life will be easier and more joyful from now on!

May 12, 2014

I get a yes to dialogue with Powerful.

EMILY. Do you have any comments for me, Powerful?

POWERFUL. Yes, I see you are uncomfortable with my presence. Please relax, and reread our first and only connection.

EMILY. I just reread our only dialogue of December 2, 2013. I feel tired and need to take a nap. Be back soon.

I take a short nap.

EMILY. I am ready to continue. Are you ready to resume, Powerful?

POWERFUL. Yes, I am. I know you take a nap about this time every day, so I am not surprised, nor do I think you are avoiding me. Yes, I am ready to continue now that you are ready.

I hear nothing.

EMILY. I do not hear any words. Please continue.

POWERFUL. I see you getting close to accepting my title as one of your aspects, but you are not happy about this. Yes?

EMILY. I am not sure what to say. I don't see how one can feel powerful and humble at the same time. Can you explain this?

POWERFUL. Yes, I would like very much to explain. True power only comes about when one is totally humble or free from being directed by the ego. Then one knows he or she is one with God and does not worry about what others think about him or her. This does not mean you do not care for others, but you are led by God thoughts. Then you are truly powerful. This is a goal of many lifetimes. For now, here today, think of power, and let the feeling of power come from a sense of connection with the divine—feeling one with all things. That is an excellent place to start. Your new work with the book *Spirituality of the Third Millennium* by Roger Lanphear will be good for you. For now, just let the word *powerful* sit quietly on your shoulders. That is close enough. I close for now.

EMILY. Thank you. I now open a dialogue with Ability to Say No. Do you have comments?

ABILITY TO SAY NO. Yes. I like the way you are giving others time frames instead of a flat no. This is a fair and powerful way to negotiate with others.

EMILY. Thank you. This is very different from our earlier dialogues.

ABILITY TO SAY NO. That is for sure, and those dialogues were from only about one year ago! Look how far you have come.

EMILY. Thank you for the kind words of encouragement.

I get a yes that I am almost through collecting all of my fractured-off parts. I am a little sad, as I have enjoyed meeting each one of

162

them. Then I hear these words inside my head: "There is still much to learn from each part, but the initial discovery phase is complete. You will soon be able to feel the joy of wholeness, which has been missing in your life."

May 26, 2014

Today I do various release processes using the script from *Feelings Buried Alive Never Die.* I never know what will come up to be released when I sit to do this work, but it always feels beneficial at the end.

EMILY. I now open a dialogue with Acceptance. Do you have comments for me?

ACCEPTANCE. Yes. Please reread our previous dialogues. It has been a while since we connected. Now do you see why it is so important for you to keep writing these dialogues? It is also important for you to do the release work, as you call it. Now for the real job of acceptance—acceptance of the fact that you are truly connecting with a real unseen world. Yes, you have the ability to do this, and you have the ability to do it with great clarity. Please allow this concept to soak into your being. You keep questioning that this is real. It is time to let that doubt go. I close for now in love and light.

EMILY. Thank you so much!

I get a yes from Intuition.

EMILY. I just reread our one and only dialogue, but I remember the words well. Please comment.

INTUITION. Oh, I love the way you are blooming. You have been a tight bud of potential for so long, and now you are gently, surely, and steadily expanding. This is lovely. You cannot see your own light, but it is steadily growing. Now for my lesson for this day. It has to do with what Acceptance said. You are on the verge of stepping into the true unknown, and we all know this is not easy for you. Please know that you are not in this alone. Your whole team is here for you, like cheerleaders. We encourage your release work and your connecting work. I might not have dialogued much, but words are not needed except to validate your intuition. You really don't need to talk to me, as I am such a part of you. All you need to do is acknowledge that you are intuitive. That is all from me as far as words. I love you!

EMILY. Oh! I love you too. So I will say it: I am intuitive! There. I even said it out loud. Do you mean there is nothing I have to do to be intuitive and stay clearly connected with my aspects?

INTUITION. Let me clarify. You are intuitive. That is a gift you were born with. To stay clearly connected requires constant vigilance, as you are watching over a sacred practice. This is a practice, not a birth gift.

EMILY. Thank you for the clarification. Is this what you mean by teaching me?

INTUITION. It is.

EMILY. Thank you again.

This is amazing. I can't believe I am doing this. Then I get a yes to dialogue with Trust and Faith in Guidance.

EMILY. This is our first dialogue, and I am exhilarated and apprehensive.

TRUST AND FAITH IN GUIDANCE. We are thrilled to be having this conversation. Oh, at last! We all had to wait for divine timing. We all know this is a real step out for you, dear Emily. But you do not know yet how important this work is that you are doing. Just know that the more you do this, the more you will learn to trust your listening skills. It is different from regular listening. Yes, we know this is confusing, but that is the best word in the English language, so we will use it at this time. We close by saying welcome aboard!

EMILY. Do you mean you are ready to integrate, or did you already integrate?

TRUST AND FAITH IN GUIDANCE. We integrated as soon as you acknowledged us on your list of aspects, but please use today's date. And we would like the usual candle ceremony too.

EMILY. I feel your enthusiasm. My apprehension is completely gone. Thank you for being with me. I love all of my aspects. I now am getting a yes to connect with my inner children. Please comment.

INNER CHILDREN. We just want to say that we all feel much safer being a part of you. We like the way you are standing up to others when needed. We feel much better and safer. Please keep it up! That is all for now, and thank you for the marvelous trip to the Oregon Coast with your girlfriends.

May 27, 2014

Today I met with a gifted energy practitioner. She helped me identify and release some limiting beliefs. I was not surprised that one belief was "I am not powerful."

Chart of Aspects as of May 26, 2014

New Name	Previous Name	Date First Noted	Date Fully Integrated
Tenacity	Rigid Taskmaster	4-7-12	5-8-12
Courage	Stern Enforcer	4-7-12	5-8-12
Flexible	Saboteur	6-4-12	1-22-13
Balanced	Defective	6-12-12	8-11-12
Beloved	Unlovable	6-12-12	9-10-12
Precious	Unworthy	6-12-12	11-6-12
Clarity	Overwhelmed and Confused	6-20-12	9-5-12
Conscience	Guilt	6-20-12	8-3-12
Organized	Perfectionist	7-9-12	8-13-12
Let It Be	Judge's Eye	7-13-12	7-13-12
Self-Assured	Sick Hospital Patient Self-Esteem	7-25-12 10-3-12	10-3-12
Safety Team and Security Force	Safety Team and Security Force	8-3-12	8-3-12
Intuition	Super-Responsible One	8-6-12	8-6-12
Joy	Sadness	8-6-12	8-6-12
Strength	Inadequate	8-11-12	8-11-12
Acceptance	Pity	8-27-12	9-5-12

Playful	Shy One	8-27-12	8-27-12
Takes Action and Connected to Source	Fear	9-10-12	9-10-12
Ability to Say No	Inability to Say No	9-11-12	5-18-13
Integrity	Anger	9-11-12	9-11-12
Guided	People Pleaser	9-12-12	7-22-13
Adventurous	Snit and Snat	9-21-12	11-6-12
Self-Compassion	High Judge	11-19-12	11-19-12
Trust and Faith in Self	Black Woman in Dream	12-12-12	5-5-14
Creative	Creative	1-23-13	1-23-13
Powerful	Powerful	12-2-13	
Trust and Faith in Guidance	Trust and Faith in Guidance	5-5-14	5-26-14

Chapter 14

The Real Work of Accepting Yourself Is Just Beginning

June 2, 2014

I USE THE SCRIPT from *Feelings Buried Alive Never Die* and ask for the release of people-pleaser traits, fear of disapproval and rejection by others, and assumption of responsibility for the feelings and behavior of others. I replace each with a positive affirmation.

Determined to release the energy of all that no longer serves me, I do a self-forgiveness process regarding trauma from my high school years involving my nonparticipation in volleyball. I feel a sense of freedom upon completion.

The nudge to use a laptop instead of handwriting my dialogues keeps coming to me. I am uncomfortable with this idea.

EMILY. I am getting a yes to open a dialogue with People Pleaser. Please begin.

PEOPLE PLEASER. I need to speak in my role as People Pleaser and not my new title of Guided. That will come later. You still have so much angst over trying to please others. I understand why you still want to be a people pleaser even as you are steadily moving away from this trait. Your progress is exciting. All of your aspects applaud the way you are beginning to let others be the way they are without trying to change them. We know this is a huge task for you, but all of us are here cheering you on. We love you!

EMILY. I love you too, and thanks for the support. I am getting a yes to open a dialogue with Acceptance. I am not sure I want to hear what you have to say, but I am willing to listen and write it down.

ACCEPTANCE. I know you are having a challenging time in accepting others in your life, but your acceptance of them will help you tremendously. I know you do not see it now, but it is in your future to do this. Completing Eckhart Tolle's book *The New World* would be helpful for you as well. As for other books on your reading list, you might want to recheck each one and ask about the benefit. Do this when you are relaxed and with your support team in place. You are wise to discern which books you spend time with, as each book has a message for you. Your own clearing and releasing of blocks and your own dialogues are just as important, if not more so. This will help you on your path to self-acceptance. I love you!

EMILY. Thank you so much for this wisdom. I now open a dialogue with my inner children. I feel you almost bursting to share with me.

INNER CHILDREN. Wheee! We are excited to be with you this day. Despite events in your life, we feel safe with you, our dear Big Emily.

EMILY. That is a relief. Thank you for the support. Please continue.

INNER CHILDREN. We know you could do your dialogues on a laptop. We are also thrilled at the acknowledgment of the pain held by High School Emily over that volleyball situation and the subsequent forgiveness and release. We all feel much better! A load has been lifted from our lives. Thank you so much! And we love the release work you are doing. Yes, it is a work of love. We also really like the Spring Forest Qigong you have been doing, and we are looking forward to a walk outside this evening. We love you.

EMILY. I am thrilled that you are thrilled. Thank you for your support. I love you!

June 9, 2014

This day I use the script and do release processes around my fear of angry people and fear of trusting due to lack of trust in self. Then I use the script to release emotions regarding various health issues.

EMILY. I am getting a yes to dialogue with Trust and Faith in Self. Please comment.

TRUST AND FAITH IN SELF. You will be able to choose a laptop for yourself. Use your own intuition as a guide. Yes, it will all work out easily. It is important that you start to have these precious dialogues in an electronic format, which will make it much easier to share your experiences with others in this time and space. Maybe you can see that you are well on your way to the real you—the one you will allow to be in the world. You have unique gifts that must be shared. Your trust in yourself and the universe is growing daily. We, your aspects, are pleased to be on this path with you. Love and blessings.

EMILY. Thank you so much for the encouragement.

For several weeks, I have been trying to merge my inner children into one Little Emily. This process worked well for John Bradshaw, as he describes in his book *Homecoming*, but it is not happening with these parts of myself.

EMILY. I now open a dialogue with Little Emily and my inner children.

LITTLE EMILY AND INNER CHILDREN. We are all jumping up and down with glee at being freed from our fear of being with angry people. Oh, this was a huge boulder removed from our life! You might be asked to do more release of this, as the issue is so big, but we all want you to know that this was huge. And no, we do not really want to merge into one Little Emily. We like being Inner Children, and one of us is Little Emily. That is because we are not all little. Some of us are your teenage self and young adult self, who do not wish to be called Little Emily.

EMILY. I hear you. And thank you for the clarification of your title and for the news of how much the release of being afraid of angry people means to you. I love that you are real and a part of me.

INNER CHILDREN. We would all like you to believe that we are real. We know you still doubt these dialogues are real, but they are, and yes, we are real too. Someday you will really know that we are real. We hope that day comes soon. Maybe you could try talking to us on days other than these wonderful Mondays.

EMILY. I hear you, and I feel your need to be recognized as a real part of me. I will ponder this. Thank you so much. I am so busy trying to clear all the blocks to living my new path that I tend to forget about you. I know you add a richness to my life. Do you have suggestions for me?

INNER CHILDREN. Yes, we want to play with color and make noise. Now that it is getting warm outside, you could take us to the old studio to play one day soon.

EMILY. That is a marvelous idea! Yes, I will do that soon. I just penciled two possible times on my calendar. This sounds like fun!

June 14, 2014

My husband recently found a sale coupon for a laptop. I now own a laptop! It all happened easily and quickly.

June 16, 2014

I use the script to continue the release of fear of angry people. Then I use the script to release the codependent traits of the fear of criticism and judgment despite the tendency to be critical and judgmental of others and the self-pressure to be a perfectionist. I feel much better after each release.

I get a yes to release emotions regarding cancer using the same release process. I connect with my support team. I feel the need for extra assistance and ask my higher self to put a light tent around me. This is a huge issue for me. Tears flow, and I do thymus EFT tapping during the release process. At last, I feel better and get a yes that all has been released at this time.

EMILY. I now open my dialogue session with People Pleaser. Please comment.

PEOPLE PLEASER. Oh, I wish you were not so engrained in my traits. You keep trying to please others without thinking of yourself. Do you remember how upset you were a few days ago until you finally realized you did not have sufficient information to make a decision? Then you relaxed and allowed a clear thought to come through, which led to an effective plan. You are coming along as fast as you are able.

EMILY. Do you have any suggestions?

PEOPLE PLEASER. You are already doing everything I have been suggesting, including releasing codependent traits. This is working for you, even though you do not see the results yet. You have been in people-pleasing mode for many years. Things are shifting rapidly. Just keep doing what you are doing.

EMILY. Thank you. I now open a dialogue with Trust and Faith in Guidance. Do you have comments?

TRUST AND FAITH IN GUIDANCE. Yes. Do you see how you are receiving and listening to hunches given throughout the day? You are wise to check these out, as you are doing. You are clearing your connections to the unseen world and will be getting more reliable hunches. This is exciting!

EMILY. Thank you for the acknowledgment.

July 3, 2014

At our session today, Georgie says she thinks my people-pleasing tendency and my fear of angry people are connected and work together. Being angry is a way some people try to control others. She suggests that when I am no longer fearful of an angry person, the person's bully energy is deflated, and he or she will either stop or go away.

July 7, 2014

I use the script for release processes around the codependent traits of harsh self-judgment and fear to trust due to lack of trust in self. Then I use the script to release emotions regarding health issues.

I cannot prove any of this is real, but I feel so much better at the end that I continue.

EMILY. I now open a dialogue with my inner children. Please comment.

INNER CHILDREN. This is amazing. We are so excited! This is such a journey, and we are glad you are taking us on this ride of a lifetime. Keep doing these dialogues and the clearing. What will be next? Who knows? This is an adventure. Bye for now. We love you.

EMILY. I love you all so much too.

August 4, 2014

Using the script, I release the codependent traits of the feeling that discovery of real self will cause rejection and the fear to trust due to lack of trust in self. Some issues seem to need a number of releases.

August 5, 2014

In our session today, Georgie says, "How much more proof do you need that this is real? Your outer life is changing for the better as well. The universe has an agenda. It is time for you to admit that this is real!"

Georgie encourages me to release doubts about the reality of my dialogues and the fear of the opinions of others. She says that when I truly know this is real, it will not matter what others say, and when I know my truth, I will be able to share these dialogues. She tells me, "Take this knowledge from my aspects to a place where I own it, heart, soul, and body." I quake inside at these words, but I stay the course and keep doing my dialogues.

August 18, 2014

Today as I call in my support team, I feel their amazing energy. It's my first day using my new laptop. I use the script to release harsh self-judgment, the feeling that discovery of real self will cause rejection, and the fear of people and authority figures. I replace each release with a positive affirmation.

EMILY. I now open a dialogue with Acceptance. Please comment.

ACCEPTANCE. This is a new way to communicate with you, dear Emily. I am sure I will get used to it soon. I want to talk to you, but first, please reread some of our last dialogues.

EMILY. I just reread our last dialogue of May 26, 2014, when you told me this work is real. Please continue.

ACCEPTANCE. Yes, and then I said the real work of accepting yourself is just beginning. Do you see how you were led to release the codependent beliefs of not loving and approving of yourself and how that release helped you to see that your use of judgment of others is actually judgment of yourself? You made a huge shift with that one insight. You also found another way of working with the script when releasing fears. This is a powerful process and will help you to grow much faster. We, your aspects, want you to love and approve of yourself. Goodbye for now, and blessings.

EMILY. Thank you for your encouragement.

I don't feel I am doing the same thing I was doing when using my pen and paper, but I keep going.

EMILY. I now open a dialogue with Trust and Faith in Self. Please comment.

TRUST AND FAITH IN SELF. We think this is fun! We like your use of the computer. See how much faster you can do the communications? Yes, this is good for us too. We can go really fast if that is called for. We just want to give you a huge blessing for your realization that all of your releasing processes are truly releasing blocked energy. And please write out the affirmation that came up four times today: "Love and approve of yourself just the way you are." Yes, *you are amazing, and we want you to believe that with every cell of your being!* Goodbye for now.

EMILY. Thank you so much. I will make a card with this affirmation.

August 19, 2014

In our session today, Georgie says that I am clearly dedicated and committed to my dialogues and that the rest of my life is my laboratory for this, my new life's work. Then she says I will be able to use what I am receiving.

Other friends have also commented that they see my dedication. This surprises me, as my dialogues take no dedication. They are fun and exciting. My aspects are helping me change my life for the better. Each time I dialogue, I feel the thrill of adventure. Who is waiting to talk? What do they have to share? What new part of me will be revealed? I am exploring an entirely new space. This does not come from a book that someone else has written. I am the first one here. It is thrilling!

September 1, 2014

A few days ago, I learned that Georgie will be retiring and moving to another state. I understand that she needs to move on with her life, but I will miss her greatly. Today I use the script to release fear of Georgie's retirement and the codependent traits of harsh self-judgment, the fear of disapproval and rejection of others, feelings of inadequacy and low self-esteem, and the fear that the discovery of real self will cause rejection. I make an affirmation card for "I love and approve of myself just the way I am."

EMILY. I begin a dialogue with Self-Assured. Please comment.

SELF-ASSURED. Please reread our last conversations.

EMILY. I reread our only two conversations of October 3, 2012, and December 3, 2012, and I feel a bit tired now.

SELF-ASSURED. There you go with that harshly judging yourself bit. I will be pleased when you let go of that codependent trait, which is so engrained in your body and mind. If I can help things along, you will let go of that trait soon. See what marvelous help from the unseen world is coming your way. You are ready for this next step, my dear Emily. Please continue this work. I just wanted to touch base with you. I have no further comments.

EMILY. Thank you for your kind words.

I don't know why, but I feel a twinge of inadequacy when talking to some of my aspects.

September 8, 2014

Four days ago, I had a dream called the Poison, in which several people became ill after drinking from a canteen and realized they had been poisoned. I use the process from the book *Unified* by Roger Lanphear to ask my higher self for the interpretation of this dream. I learn that something I am doing is not good for me, and it has to do with fear regarding my new life's purpose.

I connect with my support team and use the script to ask for release of the fear of not knowing my new life's purpose and of any blocks to knowledge of my new purpose. As I do this process, I feel tired and need to rest. I then feel sad, and tears flow. I have slight head tension and slight nausea. I do thymus tapping with one hand and make figure-eight signs with my other hand. I continue these actions as I say the release process. Finally, I feel better and know this process is complete. When finished, I always get a yes that there is nothing left to release.

I continue with the script for the release of codependent traits, plus the fear of trusting the universe for support.

EMILY. I open a dialogue with Integrity, formerly Anger. Please comment.

INTEGRITY. I am amazed at what you accomplished two days ago. You used some new material to work a miracle in your life. Do not dismiss this as a random happening. What you did was a milestone in your progress toward being a more advanced spiritual being. We, your aspects, are only here to applaud your actions. Please spell out what happened.

EMILY. I had an encounter with an angry person and had to speak forcefully to this one. That night, I wondered how I would ever get to sleep with all of my inner turmoil, so I did the anger release process from the book *Spirituality of the Third Millennium* by Roger Lanphear, and all anger quickly passed. I fell asleep right away. Do you have more comments?

INTEGRITY. Not at this time. Thank you for telling your story and allowing this to be a learning experience rather than an upsetting experience. Goodbye in love.

EMILY. Thank you. I now open a dialogue with Trust and Faith in Guidance.

TRUST AND FAITH IN GUIDANCE. We see you being uptight with the laptop. Please take a moment to acknowledge how well you are doing. This is a completely new use of technology, and it is only the third time you have used it. As with all things, relax, and see how well you are proceeding through life's latest challenge. And please say so out loud.

I do as requested.

TRUST AND FAITH IN GUIDANCE. There now. We want to say that we love how you have been listening to the hunches being sent your way by the unseen world. These hunches come not from any one being but from the whole of us who are working on your behalf these days. That is all we wish to say for this time. In love and light.

EMILY. Thank you. I open a dialogue with my inner children. Please comment.

INNER CHILDREN. We see you overworking again, but we do love all of the organic produce you are storing and cooking for us, so we try to be patient. We have never had our day on the calendar, and we keep seeing that it is not possible until October. We are patient, though, and will keep waiting.

EMILY. Thank you for understanding. I love you all.

September 9, 2014

During our session today, Georgie says, "As we become more comfortable with our inner children, we begin to trust them, and they get more playful. Then they integrate with us more, and we can trust their spontaneity."

Chapter 15

All People Come to Earth to Learn

September 22, 2014

THIS DAY I USE the script to release various emotional issues and codependent traits.

EMILY. I now open a dialogue with Judge's Eye. Please comment.

JUDGE'S EYE. Please reread our last dialogue. You can see that we had quite a deep conversation. I am here to say that you are making good progress with acceptance of yourself and others. I think your work today with the release of codependent traits will do a huge amount for you as you progress through this phase of your life. You will not always be as critical as you currently are. This is a big improvement from where you started back on July 13, 2012. I choose to talk to you from my original title, as I feel it is more appropriate for this day. I see you seeing with a critical eye as you view yourself and others. I suggest there is fear mixed with the critical eye, and you have blended fear with judgment. This is keeping you from letting go of much of your judgment of others and yourself. Thinking of this as the fear to release might be helpful to you at this time. That is all for now. Blessings to you.

EMILY. Amazing! Thank you so much for your insight and helpful comments.

September 29, 2014

I am more tired than usual this morning and find that I am not grounded and am not in positive polarity. Being in positive polarity means that energy is moving up the back side of the body and down the front (see appendix A). I have known for some time that it is beneficial to be in positive polarity, but this is the first time I've thought of checking which direction my energy is moving. I take steps to remedy the situation.

To become grounded, I visualize myself growing roots deep into the earth. To reach positive polarity, I tap my thymus and visualize my energy going up my back, over my head, down my front, and around my torso in a continuous loop. To my surprise, I immediately feel much better.

I use the script to release emotional issues, health issues, codependent traits, and the fear of sharing my dialogues with others.

EMILY. I now open a dialogue with Precious. Please comment.

PRECIOUS. It has been a long time since we dialogued, but it is always a pleasure.

EMILY. I just reread our last dialogue of December 9, 2013, and I am in awe of our conversations.

I am still tired and rest for a few minutes.

PRECIOUS. I think you were right about taking a short rest first.

EMILY. Yes, this is much better. I just realized I did not even call in my support team before beginning. I was tired.

I connect with my support team.

EMILY. Please continue.

PRECIOUS. I suggest you add feeling and visualizing the light of God around yourself when you are doing these dialogues. This will assist your connection with us, your aspects. I see you being a bit irritated at the release work you are being asked to do before you get to do your dialogues. I wish to explain further that not only is the clearing necessary for you at this time, but also, the powerful affirmations coming through you are of immense help to you and will be to others. They are powerful words that carry much vital meaning. These words along with your use of them will pave the way for expanded joy in your life. All you have to do is allow this joy. I close for now in love and light.

EMILY. Thank you so much.

Prompted by these comments, I develop appendix B to give examples of some of the releases and affirmations I have been using.

EMILY. I now open a dialogue with Fear.

FEAR. You did not expect to hear from me, did you? I am always with you, as that is the way things are in your life at this time. There are healthy fears, yes? I am here to talk about the ones that are not so healthy, and I see you have been doing a fine job of releasing some of these inappropriate fears. Let's go beyond that. You now realize that all people come to Earth to learn something. This is true; otherwise, coming here would be a waste of time and energy. Please allow yourself and others to have their learning experiences and honor them with love, acceptance, and maybe even a little joy. Yes, that seems a strange word to use here, but it is true. Life's lessons can be made in joy and not always in sorrow. The latter is just how most of you are used to looking at them. You equate life lessons with hard work, sadness, and stress, but who said that was true? Only other people, and what do they know? That is all I am ready to say at this time. I close in love and light.

EMILY. Thank you. I expected you to say more about the inappropriate fears.

FEAR. No. Others are doing that for me nicely.

EMILY. Thank you. I remember the last times we talked, and this was much easier.

FEAR. See? That is progress toward release of inappropriate fears.

EMILY. Thank you again. I now open a dialogue with Trust and Faith in Guidance.

TRUST AND FAITH IN GUIDANCE. Well, here we are, and we see a bit of light coming from your countenance that says you are beginning to trust that you are really receiving honest, powerful, and helpful guidance. As an aspect of you, we would like to be especially clear that you really are receiving true guidance; it is not a figment of your imagination. We are aspects of you, and we are just as real as you are. We were created to be a part of this lifetime of yours. You created us to have the experiences you knew would benefit you. It was all done for the first time too, as there is no one just like you, so it is all unique and fresh. Isn't that a fine thought? We think so. We close for now in love and light.

EMILY. Just when I think I know what you are going to say. Well, I should know by now that's not how it works. Thank you for the unique message. I now open a dialogue with my inner children.

INNER CHILDREN. We like all of the release work you are doing, and we like going on journeys with you, such as our recent trip to Yellowstone Park. We really liked that! It was a great time to really feed our being. We are also able to wait until you have more time for us. It would be nice if you could carve out a day to play with us. We think you would be surprised at what would happen, and we are not as frightened as we used to be now that you are releasing so many inappropriate fears. Thank you. We close in laughter and giggles.

EMILY. Thank you for your wise words. I appreciate your wisdom and your humor. Yes. I will carve out a day for us. You are right—I can't imagine what we would do, so it will be a surprise. I love you. I now open a dialogue with Joy.

JOY. I see that you did not really want to talk to me. In fact, I see it when you sigh in relief that I do not choose to talk to you much. I see that you made a comment today that you were not comfortable with even the word *joy*. Isn't that interesting? Food for thought. Maybe this is one of the inappropriate fears. Just a comment. I am not giving you a hard time for not having more fun in your life. I do see, though, that you are making slow but steady progress toward your goal of feeling more joyful in this lifetime. That is a goal you started out with a long time ago. You just forgot it was there. I am here to remind you. That is all. I love you so much.

EMILY. I don't know what to say. You aspects always know everything I think and feel. I guess you really are a part of me after all. Thank you for not giving me a hard time about the lack of joy.

I am doing the best I can. I appreciate that you see some slight improvement. I love you too.

October 10–13, 2014

I attend Sonia Choquette's Trust Your Vibes, Level 3 workshop. It is an incredible experience.

October 20, 2014

I use the script and ask my support team to help me release codependent traits and emotions regarding health issues.

EMILY. I now open a dialogue with Flexible. Please comment.

FLEXIBLE. This is indeed an honor. It has been a long time since we talked. Thank you for rereading our last dialogue. You have made many changes since that time, but few of those changes included flexibility. I hope you are interested at this time, as I would like to be a more regular part of the team. I joined a long time ago. It was exciting to me to see you ask your body if she wanted to do yoga for three days recently, and with prompting, you followed through with that practice. Your body wants more movement and stretching and relaxing of her muscles. This will be helpful for you today and in the years to come—and there will be years to come. Why not combine all of the great health-related practices you are now doing with the gentle movements of yoga? I close in love and smiles.

EMILY. Thank you so much, Flexible! I am looking forward to your help with this suggestion and finding the right and perfect yoga teacher for me. I now open a dialogue with Precious. Please comment.

PRECIOUS. I want to also make a suggestion. Please listen to the thumb drive from your recent Sonia Choquette event to feel the love from your higher self and all of us who love you here in the unseen world. You had a powerful experience of this love, and we wish for you to experience it on a regular basis. Just feel the love, and allow it to travel in and around your lovely body. That is all from me for this day. I love you so!

EMILY. Thank you, Precious, for the suggestion. I look forward to basking in this love. I now open a dialogue with Strength.

STRENGTH. Please reread our dialogue. Didn't really think you would ever hear from me again, did you? Well, I am here. I have not left you, and I have not forgotten our connection.

EMILY. I just reread our brief and only dialogue on August 11, 2012. That was a long time ago. Something is afoot here with all of these aspects from long ago relating to my body showing up today. Please continue.

STRENGTH. That is because of the opening you gave yourself at the Sonia Choquette event when you asked your body if she wanted to go to yoga in the morning. If she did, you said, she would wake you up at seven thirty in time to attend. Sure enough, you did wake up, and even though you checked again, you did get up and go to the yoga class. It was fun, and you were surprised you could follow along quite well.

EMILY. Yes, that all did happen. I tried two times to get out of going—I was still on Pacific time, which was five thirty, and the event was on central time—but my body kept saying she wanted to go, so I attended. Then I surprised myself, as I could do most of the exercises. I hardly ever ask my body what she wants to do. Will you help me to do yoga, Strength? And will you help me get to yoga class?

STRENGTH. I am here to help you, and I am a part of you, so let's give it a go. Start easy with low demands on yourself. Once a week is a great start, and a good teacher will be a big help. You will find the right one. Thank you again for listening today. Just stop now, and feel my power inside your body. You are a strong woman indeed. It is time you acknowledged that. You have a strong body. Love her. Talk to her. She has much to say to you.

EMILY. Now this is getting wild. Is this Physical Body you are referring to?

STRENGTH. Yes, it is Physical Body. You have worked much with Emotional Body, Spiritual Body, and Mental Body but little with Physical Body. I do not mean taking yourself out for a hike or a walk; rather, I mean asking her what she needs, as you did a day ago with the yoga class. Thank you, and yes, I will help you in all of these endeavors.

Chapter 16

Emotions Are to
Be Experienced,
Not Kept Inside

October 26, 2014, Silver Falls Retreat, Day 1

I TAKE MYSELF ON a four-day retreat to lovely Silver Falls State Park and stay in a small heated cabin. It is wonderful. I have privacy and space to dive into my work. On my drive here, I am treated to a double rainbow in the sky. I wonder what adventures await.

As I work this first evening, I ask for release of the codependent trait of harsh self-judgment and replace it with the affirmation "I love and appreciate myself." Then I play with my inner children.

October 27, 2014, Silver Falls Retreat, Day 2

Last night, I had a dream in which I felt love flowing through my body. This morning, I have this thought: *Could feeling love flowing through my body be a key to feeling safe in my body?* I don't know, but I will give it a try.

I use the book *Unconditional Forgiveness* by Mary Hayes Grieco to do forgiveness processes with any uncomfortable situation that comes to mind. It is quite a day. There are many situations. I find forgiveness work intense during the process and completely freeing at the end.

Next, I ask for release of the fear that if someone gets angry, it means he or she doesn't love me. This is bigger than the fear of angry people, which I have been trying to release with mixed success. Then I have this insight: anger does not even have to be directed at me; in the face of any anger, I immediately feel unloved and unsafe and switch to defense mode. I am terrified by anger!

Honoring this new information, I revise my wording and ask my support team to please help me release my reaction to anger—that is, when I detect any anger I feel unloved and unsafe, and switch to defense mode. Finally, I feel relief and know the process is complete.

EMILY. Despite some fear, I now open a dialogue with Anger.

ANGER. We have already been through this before, and you found a positive side to me: Integrity. I have no idea why you are so afraid of anger. It is just one of many possible emotions that humans have. No worries. Just let it flow through you, much like the love you are being advised to allow to flow. Anyway, I had to say something first before you went into fear over the sound of the word *anger*. There. I said it again. It is only an emotion, and emotions are to be experienced, not kept inside oneself. That is all I have to say at this time. I give you my best.

EMILY. Thank you for the comments. They do help. I now open a dialogue with my inner children.

INNER CHILDREN. Whoa! That was a big one. When you began to work on anger, we were afraid of what was going to happen.

189

We want to say that we are really excited about all that did happen. We feel safer and calmer than we have for a long time. Please work some more on this anger issue. We do not think it is finished yet. We don't even need to play with colors tonight. We just want to be held and loved and to know that we are safe in our body.

EMILY. Yes, this is huge, and I appreciate your saying so. I will hold you tonight, as I feel you are safely with me. I love you all so much. Thank you again. I now open a dialogue with People Pleaser.

PEOPLE PLEASER. Thank you for using my former title. It suits me at this time. Your reactions to anger play a huge role in your people-pleasing traits. If it were not for your fears, feelings of being unloved, and subsequent defense methods, you would be able to release people-pleasing in a big way. I look forward to seeing some movement in this area.

October 28, 2014, Silver Falls Retreat, Day 3

These release processes feel good when they are complete. I can't help but think that doing them is really helping my body and my life. Why not let go of the things that are not serving me?

Today I use the script and ask my support team to help me release my coping mechanism of being invisible. As soon as I say these words, I feel a tightening in my abdomen. I know by now that this is only a part of the process, so I stay the course and repeat my request.

I realize that being invisible is a lifelong pattern. It is the easy way out. I can hide out in the shadows of life, and no one will notice me. However, it is not a satisfying way, and it brings no joy. Suddenly, I feel overwhelmed with sadness and self-pity. I think self-pity is a hallmark of the invisible. As I continue with this release, my throat is tight, and I feel slightly nauseated. I move around the room and make sad sounds from my throat. I hug my inner children and repeat my request. I feel sadness releasing from every cell of my body.

Suddenly, I am afraid. What will happen if I am not invisible?

Determined to release sadness and self-pity, however, I continue this process. On a hunch, I ask if I have a fear of being visible, and I get a yes. I now include the release of the fear of being visible. After many sobs, a tight throat, and head tension, I begin to feel better. Then I feel much better and know my process is complete. I have no idea how this works, but it does work, and it works consistently.

I ask for my next priority. To my amazement, it turns out to be to welcome two-and-a-half-year-old Little Emily back. I find this curious, as an intuitive friend recently told me I almost left this earth plane at that age. I also remember reading in my baby book that at two and a half years old, I had a high fever of unknown origin.

I connect with my support team and ask about this. I hear, "Yes, it is true, and you were not really welcomed back. In fact, no one even realized you almost left. Please repair this, and give Little Emily a huge welcome and loving hugs."

I have no idea how to proceed, so I feel my way into the situation. I imagine my inner children as though they are actually present. First, I hug Little Emily and tell her how glad I am that she decided to come back. I tell her I know it was a big decision and am honored she made this choice. I tell her I love her very much.

I make a huge drawing with colored pencils in my notebook. In the center of the page is two-and-a-half-year-old Little Emily, and all around her are my other inner children and Big Emily. We are all sending her love and telling her how glad we are that she is back. Then I hold all of my inner children in a big imaginary hug and tell each one that I love her very much. I draw a rainbow across the top of my notebook picture and write, "Welcome back, two-and-a-half-year-old Little Emily!"

At last, I feel I have integrated with my own inner children. I laugh, as this was a goal of John Bradshaw's book *Homecoming*, which I previously thought was not possible. I now feel both whole and a part of each inner child at the same time. It is grand and complete.

My next priority is to release my inability to say no. Despite the fact that this trait has negatively affected my life and that I have done this release process on two other retreats, I know I am not complete. With much anxiety, I begin again. I take out a large piece of paper and colored pastels. Then I shout, "No!" as I write the word *No* on the page. I continue with gusto. It is freeing to shout, "No!" while letting the words jump from the pastel in my hand onto a piece of paper.

Then things start going slowly, and I am stalled. An idea comes to me to try a technique I recently learned from the book *Unified* by Roger Lanphear. The technique is to ask your higher self to clear uninvited influences.

I follow the suggestion. The moment I finish the technique, I have the insight that just because I have integrated with my aspect Ability to Say No does not mean I know how to say no. This is something I am learning, and it will take time. I am overcome with sadness. This is not an easy release. All I can do is surrender to the process. I let go, and finally, I feel better. I know I've released as much as possible at this time.

My next priority is integration with my spiritual body. On January 14, 2013, I embarked on a self-forgiveness process in which my emotional and mental bodies asked for and received forgiveness from my physical body (see chapter 9). At the end of this process, I joined with my physical, emotional, and mental bodies in feeling the unconditional love of the universe.

I now know that my spiritual body needs to join with us in this love and that I need to ask forgiveness from these four parts of my body. Using the forgiveness process from Mary Hayes Grieco's book *Unconditional Forgiveness*, I follow where my intuition leads in this unique situation.

EMILY. My dear Physical Body, I now ask your forgiveness, as I am only just beginning to ask you what you need. Please forgive me for such a lack of trust in your knowledge. Do you care to respond?

PHYSICAL BODY. Yes, I would like to respond. I am thrilled at the way you listened to me and took us to yoga the other day and for asking about my needs two other times. Of course I forgive you. I do hope this is the beginning of a long and fruitful relationship. I look forward to this becoming a part of your life. I can really help, you know.

EMILY. This was not what I was expecting. Thank you for speaking up easily. During our first dialogue on January 14, 2013, you did not even know you had a voice. I sense huge healing on your part. Thank you for this acknowledgment and forgiveness. I look forward to your help.

I move on to the next part of me.

EMILY. My dear Emotional Body, I now ask your forgiveness for only beginning to allow you to express certain feelings. I know I have more to do in this area. On January 14, 2013, you said you had been repressed for much of our life, and I would like to ask if the release-of-emotions process is helpful [see chapter 14].

EMOTIONAL BODY. Yes, I do forgive you, dear Emily, and yes, the emotional release process is amazing. It is helpful for me, as are the recent anger and fear releases you are doing. Please continue, and thank you for asking. I especially like the comments made last night by Anger.

EMILY. Thank you so much. It helps to be acknowledged.

I move on to the next part.

EMILY. My dear Mental Body, I now ask your forgiveness for the continued pressure I put on you. I am trying to do things differently, like being in my heart and being spirit-led, but these are new concepts for me. Do you care to respond?

MENTAL BODY. Yes, I would like to respond. I do forgive you, and I would like to be asked for suggestions once in a while. That is all I have to say.

EMILY. Thank you for your forgiveness and for your response. You will not lose your place with me as we become spirit-led. In fact, that is when things will finally start to lighten up for you. You will be free to be who you were really created to be.

Finally, I address Spiritual Body.

EMILY. My dear Spiritual Body, I now ask your forgiveness for so many years of being unaware of you in my life. I am only now catching glimpses of who and what you really are, and I am amazed. I don't even know if you are a real part of my body, and I do not remember what prompted me to include you today. Do you care to respond?

SPIRITUAL BODY. Of course I would like to respond. There is nothing to forgive, as you did not know of my existence until today. Yes, I am a real part of our body, and yes, I can be a huge help. Please consider calling on me with questions and concerns. I am the one most closely linked to our higher self. Thank you for this acknowledgment.

EMILY. Thank you for your response.

I move to a self-forgiveness process. At the end, I ask my physical, emotional, mental and spiritual bodies to join with me in feeling the unconditional love of the universe. It is a heartfelt experience.

EMILY. I now open a dialogue with Connected to Source, formerly a part of Fear. Please comment.

CONNECTED TO SOURCE. Hello. This is almost the only time we have held a dialogue. I am honored to speak with you this fine evening. I have been listening and watching intently as you connect with your higher self for guidance, feel the love of the universe, and dialogue with your spiritual body. These are all examples of being connected to Source. These connections will aid you in living a spirit-led life if that is what you truly want. Think about this before you move on, as it is a very different way of living life. Maybe the words came out by accident, but I think not. I close for now in love and light.

EMILY. Thank you so much. It is also an honor to dialogue with you. I think that being spirit-led is what I do want in life, though. I now open a dialogue with Ability to Say No.

ABILITY TO SAY NO. You did a great job today with releasing more facets of your inability to say no. I would like to suggest that you also use another modality, such as the *Spirituality of the Third Millennium* book by Roger Lanphear. And you will need to be diligent in your release of fear around anger if you really want to get to the bottom of that issue. That is all I have for now. I am on your side and wish to be of help, in case you have doubts.

EMILY. Thank you. I appreciate your suggestions. I now open a dialogue with my inner children.

INNER CHILDREN. Wheee! This was a grand day for all of us. We feel blessed at this family reunion. We did not realize what a painful experience it was for two-and-a-half-year-old Little Emily when no one even noticed she left her physical body and then decided to come back. She has been in pain for a long time. We think you will feel differently about us from now on, and we will be a more normal part of you from this day forth. We love you!

EMILY. I love you too. Thank you for being here with me at this time. I feel calm about all of you. The usual anxiety over how to parent you is not here today. I am grateful.

I am learning that nurturing my inner children is a gateway to my adult self, who also longs for nurturing.

October 29, 2014, Silver Falls Retreat, Day 4

At a recent Sonia Choquette event, Trust Your Vibes, Level 3, we were asked to release a part of ourselves we no longer needed. To my surprise, the name Fraidy Cat came to me. This was a cartoon character from my childhood who was afraid of everything.

Today I begin steps to release Fraidy Cat. On a hunch, I ask about this release, and I get a response that I can release as much as I am willing to let go of today. I use the script release process and discover much fear underneath the surface. Finally, I feel better and know the process is complete at least for now.

My last priority is to integrate with my aspects. I call in my support team and proceed. I am in uncharted waters. I have never read or heard of anyone doing what I am doing. I go deep inside and allow a process to unfold.

I relax and visualize each aspect getting close to my body.

I call on and acknowledge each one. As I do so, I hear comments and feel sensations. Some aspects even tell me they are not really aspects and wish to be removed from my list.

With each acknowledgment, I feel an energy merge with my body. It is an incredible experience! Here is the result:

ACKNOWLEDGMENT OF ASPECTS

TENACITY. Honored to be on the team.

COURAGE. Honored to be on the team.

FLEXIBLE. Honored to be on the team.

BALANCED. I am different from Calm and Centered.

I am puzzled, as I rarely feel calm and centered, so I wait for a response.

CALM AND CENTERED. I am a missing aspect.

EMILY. Thank you. Welcome to the team.

I add this new aspect to my list.

BELOVED. Ahaaaaa.

The sound from Beloved is like a loving sigh.

PRECIOUS. This was God's name for me. You know you are now directly connected to God.

As Precious merges with my body, I feel a huge sense of peace.

I hear nothing from Clarity, but I feel myself coming out of the fog as Clarity tiptoes in.

CONSCIENCE. I am not an aspect but something that is just here.

I remove Conscience from my aspect list.

I hear nothing from Organized, but I know Perfectionist, the former title of Organized, still shows up on occasion, so this is an aspect of mine.

LET IT BE. I am not an aspect but something that is just here.

I remove Let It Be from my aspect list.

I hear nothing from Self-Assured, but I feel amazingly strong in my body.

I hear laughter from Safety Team and Security Force.

INTUITION. My name is really Intuitive.

I make this change on my list. I feel a whoosh of energy as Intuitive merges.

I hear laughter from Joy.

JOY. Joy is not the opposite of sadness but different. Sadness is part of acceptance of humanness. I, Joy, am one of your aspects.

I am able to complete this process with only half of my aspects, as it is checkout time for the cabin. I plan to finish as soon as possible.
I never know what will happen or what I will hear when I connect with these parts of myself. It is a true adventure! As I close this amazing retreat, I feel a sense of wholeness I have never felt before.

Chart of Aspects as of October 29, 2014

New Name	Previous Name	Date First Noted	Date Fully Integrated
Tenacity	Rigid Taskmaster	4-7-12	5-8-12
Courage	Stern Enforcer	4-7-12	5-8-12
Flexible	Saboteur	6-4-12	1-22-13
Balanced	Defective	6-12-12	8-11-12
Calm and Centered		10-29-14	10-29-14
Beloved	Unlovable	6-12-12	9-10-12
Precious	Unworthy	6-12-12	11-6-12
Clarity	Overwhelmed and Confused	6-20-12	9-5-12
Organized	Perfectionist	7-9-12	8-13-12
Self-Assured	Sick Hospital Patient Self-Esteem	7-25-12 10-3-12	10-3-12
Safety Team and Security Force	Safety Team and Security Force	8-3-12	8-3-12
Intuitive	Super-Responsible One	8-6-12	8-6-12
Joy	Sadness	8-6-12	8-6-12
Strength	Inadequate	8-11-12	8-11-12
Acceptance	Pity	8-27-12	9-5-12

Playful	Shy One	8-27-12	8-27-12
Takes Action and Connected to Source	Fear	9-10-12	9-10-12
Ability to Say No	Inability to Say No	9-11-12	5-18-13
Integrity	Anger	9-11-12	9-11-12
Guided	People Pleaser	9-12-12	7-22-13
Adventurous	Snit and Snat	9-21-12	11-6-12
Self-Compassion	High Judge	11-19-12	11-19-12
Trust and Faith in Self	Black Woman in Dream	12-12-12	5-5-14
Creative	Creative	1-23-13	1-23-13
Powerful	Powerful	12-2-13	
Trust and Faith in Guidance	Trust and Faith in Guidance	5-5-14	5-26-14

LOVE

Chapter 17

The Love Your Aspects
Have for You

November 3, 2014

USING THE DREAM-INTERPRETATION PROCESS from *Unified* by Roger Lanphear, I ask my higher self to please reveal the meaning of a recent dream, Floodwaters. In this dream, I was standing on a wooden garden terrace and saw floodwaters below my feet, surging under the boards.

HIGHER SELF. You are moving into your subconscious. It feels overwhelming. As you release the fear of connection with the subconscious, you will see the danger leaving.

Then I ask about my dream Telling Family I'm Pregnant, in which I told my family I was pregnant but wondered how that was possible, as I had not ovulated for years.

HIGHER SELF. You are excited about and beginning to use some of the new ways of transforming your life. You question how this is possible. You continue to play in the subconscious without true awareness.

These dreams give me the incentive to continue releasing uncomfortable issues. I feel my life transforming for the better.

I use the script to release the codependent trait of feeling inadequate and having low self-esteem and replace it with the affirmations "I am worthy of God's love" and "I receive God's love."

I continue with release of my fear of failure despite my tendency to sabotage my own success and replace it with "There is no right or wrong way, just a different path."

This entire process amazes me, and I continue with more releases. Each one feels like a beneficial thing to do for my body.

I then use the script to release emotions regarding health issues, including cancer. This last one is scary, but I replace it with "I lovingly forgive and release my past" and "I love and appreciate myself."

EMILY. I now open a dialogue with my inner children.

INNER CHILDREN. We are still basking in the new feeling of being integrated since the Silver Falls retreat and the wholeness of having two-and-a-half-year-old Little Emily welcomed at last. It was a marvelous time. We close in satisfaction and peace.

November 10, 2014

An intuitive friend recently told me that two-and-a-half-year-old Little Emily is still angry. Today I find myself being upset about another issue as well. I get a yes that being upset is the closest I get to anger, and I realize how fearful I am of expressing anger. I am unsure how to proceed. I get a no to using the script and a yes to asking my support team to do the release instead.

First, I check to be sure there are no cars parked close to the building, as I never know how much noise I will make when I start releasing things. It looks clear, so I ask my support team to please help me release anger from two-and-a-half-year-old Little Emily and my other issue. My head feels tense. I rock back and forth while doing EFT tapping. Anger is not an easy emotion for me to allow. I make some anger sounds and stomp around the room, allowing the feeling of anger to flow through my being. I am surprised I can actually feel energy moving inside myself. Soon I feel better and know that some long-stuck anger has been released from my body.

Excited at the discovery of my own way to release stuck anger, I can't help but proceed. I try this new process on other anger situations. As I begin, I have the following insight: "This does not mean the other person needs to agree with me. All I am doing is expressing an emotion called anger."

I feel sudden head tension and realize a part of me does not want to do this release process, but I know it is the only way to get the tension to release, so I continue. I repeat my new process of asking my support team to assist in the release. I make anger sounds and stomp around the room. Suddenly, I feel an energy move through my body, and I feel much better.

Then I have another insight: "I do not even need to tell the other person I am angry. I only need to feel the energy of this emotion move through my cells."

I learn this is what it feels like to allow the emotion of anger to flow through my body. At the end, I feel calm and complete with this adventure.

EMILY. I now open a dialogue with Sadness.

SADNESS. I am a feeling that is to be felt and allowed to move through your body. For many years now, you have held me as a part of you. Sadness was stuck in you for so long I became a part of you. Now that you are learning to move stuck emotions through and out of your body, you will not need to have me as an aspect. I have enjoyed being a part of you, but I know it is best that I move along. I suggest you do a ceremony of saying goodbye with your candles. Interesting, isn't it, this working with aspects? I close for now in love and light.

EMILY. It certainly is interesting. I never know what I will hear or feel. Thank you for sharing.

I check my notes from my Silver Falls retreat in October 2014 and learn that joy is not the opposite of sadness but different, and sadness is part of the acceptance of being human. Sadness originally showed up for me as an aspect, but its role has changed now that I've allowed the feelings to flow. I have a candle ceremony to say goodbye to my former aspect Sadness. It seems my list of aspects is a fluid, changing entity.

EMILY. I now open a dialogue with Little Emily and my inner children.

LITTLE EMILY AND INNER CHILDREN. We really liked the anger work you did today! It is new for us to be feeling this again after so long. You have been angry, but you did not allow the feelings to move through your body, as you were tightly holding on to control and the fear of being angry. Did you think you were going to burst if you allowed anger to flow? It is okay, as you are now beginning to find out what it feels like to feel anger and realizing you can feel anger without losing control of yourself. It will take some time and practice, but this is a great start. We love you, and we are excited, as this process frees up a lot of closely bound-up energy that was inside your body.

EMILY. This is amazing! I will see how I feel in the future. Thank you. I love you all.

November 17, 2014

This day I use my new process of asking my support team to release various codependent traits and to release anger over various life situations.

Then I get a yes that I need to especially welcome back two-and-a-half-year-old Little Emily. I see her in my mind's eye and hold her in my arms as I rock her gently and say, "I love you unconditionally." I tell her she can have all the feelings she wants, I am here for her, and it is safe to be in our body.

In the past, I felt anxious and uncertain about how to parent my own inner children, but today I feel calm and relaxed. I find myself saying, "I am strong and able to protect you, Little Emily." I open my notebook and draw a picture of Little Emily wrapped in a purple blanket inside a ring of glowing orange light. I say, "You are safe. I am safe. It is safe to be in our body. I love you! Our higher self loves you! God loves you! There is nothing you can ever do to change that. Nothing."

EMILY. I now open a dialogue with Precious.

PRECIOUS. Emily, you cannot imagine the love we, your aspects, all have for you. You barely think we are real. Someday—we hope soon—you will begin to allow some of our love for you to enter your body. For now, we say please allow the love to flow through your body. We close in love and more love.

EMILY. It always amazes me to hear you say things like this. I think I am open to your love, yet I am not sure. Thank you for your kind words. I now open a dialogue with Strength.

STRENGTH. Do you see how you handled the situation yesterday when you were physically helping to clear clutter from a friend's house and started to feel unwell? You listened to your body and realized you needed to release uninvited influences. You asked your support team for assistance, and you felt better after the energy was released. This is strength. Strength is not limited to the physical body. Strength exists in all phases of being human and spiritual at the same time. I close in love, peace, and joy.

EMILY. Oh, thank you very much. This is encouraging. I now open a dialogue with Joy.

JOY. We are delighted to be with you this day! Do you feel how we each have our own energy? Does this help you to see and feel that we are real energies? Joy is a unique energy. We would like you to begin to feel more of it in your human body. It might seem odd because this is not a feeling you are accustomed to. Joy was not something you embraced in many of your lifetimes. It is quite new for you, which is why you are feeling as if you will never be able to feel its wonders. Relax. Calm down, and let this soak in. This is meant not as criticism but as a helpful comment. We close in joy!

EMILY. I long for joy to be a part of my life. I think it is beginning. Thank you for your helpful suggestions. I close with smiles and calmness. I now open a dialogue with Little Emily and my inner children.

LITTLE EMILY AND INNER CHILDREN. We love all the releasing you did today. Thank you! We all feel much safer than before. We keep feeling safer and safer. It is grand! Thank you again. Maybe someday we can play more.

EMILY. I know you keep reminding me gently that playing is great. It is like being in joy. Both are foreign to me. I know this will come to pass one of these days. Thank you for understanding. I love you.

November 24, 2014

Today I use Mary Hayes Grieco's *Unconditional Forgiveness* to do self-forgiveness for my inability to say no. During the process, I get an insight that the entire issue really centers on my fear of anger. At the end, I feel much better. Self-forgiveness really works!

When I was nine years old, I fainted after a smallpox immunization given at my school and was unconscious for several minutes. Recently, an energy-healer friend said something happened at that time and suggested I welcome back my nine-year-old self, as I did my two-and-a-half-year-old self. Again, there is no how-to book for this, so I create my own welcome-back ceremony similar to the one I did for Little Emily.

In my mind's eye, I picture myself leaning over my nine-year-old self. She is lying on a table in the school lunchroom and has just regained consciousness. I whisper in low tones, "Welcome back, my dear Emily. I love you. I am glad you came back to be with me. I love you so much. There is no reason to be embarrassed about fainting with your sensitive body. You are a dear, precious child of God, who loves you very much. My inner children and I welcome you back. We will always be here for you whenever you need us."

I light a candle in honor of this event and draw a picture in my notebook of nine-year-old Emily in a blue dress with an orange bubble around herself. Love is flowing to her from God and all of my inner children. I write in big blue letters above the picture, "Welcome back, nine-year-old Emily!"

This is the first time I have had the thought to include God in a ceremony.

EMILY. I now open a dialogue with Ability to Say No.

ABILITY TO SAY NO. I am pleased to speak today. I see you releasing the old baggage you were dragging along behind you in all of these situations where you were not able to say no in the past. Yes, it is time to cut the cords and release this extra drag on your life and your body. Each time you release one of these bowling balls of negativity, you help yourself and those around you. Thank you. I close for today in pride and purpose.

EMILY. Thank you so much. I appreciate the confirmation that it is worth the effort. I now open a dialogue with Little Emily and my inner children. Please share.

LITTLE EMILY AND INNER CHILDREN. We are pleased to be one step closer to wholeness with the welcome of nine-year-old Emily. This was not the same as two-and-a-half-year-old Little Emily's near-death experience, but it was needed. The addition of God's welcome is profound. We feel safer with each passing day. Please continue this fine work, and remember, you need to play sometimes too. We love you!

EMILY. Oh, I keep forgetting about the playing part. Thank you for your comments. I now open a dialogue with Powerful. I will admit I twitched a bit when I got a yes from you. Please comment.

POWERFUL. Yes, I felt the twitch when you saw my yes signal. One of these days, I see you feeling just as naturally about me as you do about all the others on the team. We are a team, and it takes all the players doing and being their best to make a great team. If one is absent, the team suffers. I want to say that being powerful is not as scary as you might think. In fact, it is a natural part of being made in the likeness of God. You are just not used to the idea. Sit with this knowledge, and let it soak in. You let other aspects soak in, so do the same with me. Every so often, whisper to yourself, "I am powerful." I can feel your hesitation, which is why you should do it softly at first. That is all I have to contribute today. I close in love and peace.

EMILY. Thank you. I appreciate your kind words of encouragement.

December 8, 2014

I use the script to release several codependent traits and replace each with a strong, positive affirmation. As I am releasing the fear of loving and being loved, I suddenly get a hunch to ask if this fear has to do with God. I get a yes. Surprised yet trusting my guidance, I use the script to release the fear of loving God and being loved by God. I replace this with the affirmation "I feel completely loved by God, and I totally love God."

I use the script to release my fear of anger and replace it with "I allow myself to express anger appropriately" and "The anger of others has no effect on me, as it is their feeling, not mine."

Then I release my fear to trust the universe for support and replace it with "I completely trust the universe for my support." These are strong words. When the release finally happens, it is like a bubble bursting around me, with joy filling in the spaces.

EMILY. I now open a dialogue with my inner children.

INNER CHILDREN. Oh, this is such fun. The joy that bubbled over several times today is delicious! We bask in joy. This is real joy, not fluffy, silly joy, although that is good sometimes too. We just want to say that we are happy. That is all. We close in love and more joy.

EMILY. I am pleased to learn this. I am trying to remember to love and hug you every night. It is such a joy to hug each of you. Thank you for sharing today. I now open a dialogue with Beloved.

BELOVED. Just feel these words: "Beloved. Beloved. Beloved. You are my beloved. I am your beloved." Let them soak into your being. Do not ever doubt again that you are not loved or cared for by a loving God. We think you are ready to really embrace these words and the feeling of being loved. You are ready to do this on your own. Yes, that is the truth. I close in absolute love.

EMILY. Thank you for your wonderful words. I will let this soak in. I hardly know what to say to those deep words. I love you too, my beloved.

December 15, 2014

I get a yes to release emotions regarding issues with various organs of my body. This time, however, I get a no to using the script and a yes to writing my own. I connect with my support team and key in my new release process, which comes easily and quickly (see appendix C).

Recently, this thought came to me: *My physical body is a burden.* I use my new release process to release this unhelpful thought and replace it with the affirmation "I thoroughly enjoy and appreciate being in my physical body." When my body finally relaxes, I know the process is complete.

My new release process works wonderfully, and I am grateful.

EMILY. I now open a dialogue with Tenacity.

TENACITY. I am thrilled to talk to you this day. You are over the top when it comes to Tenacity. I just want you to know how much I love you and how proud I am to be on the team! That is all.

EMILY. I am thrilled to hear from you as well. I am proud to have you on the team. I love you!

Smiles and laughter follow on both sides.

EMILY. I now open a dialogue with Joy.

JOY. I too am thrilled. You do not let me out to be thrilled often, but I see that changing. Joy has been bubbling up in all kinds of places, and I am thrilled you are allowing me to move in your body once more. When your two girls were young, you let joy move much more freely. It is time to allow joy to move again. Please heed this advice. I love you so much!

EMILY. Thank you, and I love you too. I too am thrilled at your bubbling up in the most unexpected places. I now open a dialogue with Precious.

PRECIOUS. Oh, dear one, I wish to be an encourager for you this day. You are just beginning to experience your gifts that have been slumbering for many years. It is a delight to see you doing these dialogues and to be a part of the unfolding of the real you. You have real gifts, and the more confidence you feel with them, the more they will manifest through you. You do not need to save the world, but you can make some contributions that will help many who will come to appreciate what you have to offer. Do not be afraid to use your gifts and let your light shine. I close in love and light.

EMILY. Thank you for your encouragement. I love you too. I now open a dialogue with Acceptance.

ACCEPTANCE. Do not be concerned about all these changes in your list of aspects. We all knew the list would change as you grew and changed, so please accept the list and all of us as we grow and change with you. Now that you are allowing feelings to move more freely through your body, you do not need to have those feelings as aspects. At this point comes the big work of really accepting us and allowing us to be real aspects of who you are. You are currently keeping some of us at arm's length, such as myself, and I include the acceptance of those persons you judge harshly, including yourself. Now is the opportunity to allow the best of each of us to be active in you. We love you, or we would not be saying any of these things. Blessings today.

EMILY. I need to reread and think about what you said. I want all of this. I relax in your loving words. I now open a dialogue with my inner children.

INNER CHILDREN. We want to say that we feel safer than before. We do not feel you being as afraid, and that is wonderful. You have more to do in the area of safety, but it is coming, and we are relieved, or we will be soon. That is all we have to say—well, except that we would like to play with color soon.

EMILY. I hear you. I will make this a priority after the holidays.

Chapter 18

Joy Is a Feeling of Well-Being No Matter What Is Going On In the Outer World

December 29, 2014

I GET A YES to continue my release of the thought that my physical body is a burden (see December 15, 2014). Using my new release process (see appendix C), I find myself going deeper this second time and including releases of feeling unworthy, feeling that things are impossible, feeling too old, not knowing enough, feeling incapable, having already pushed my body to the limit, and ignoring my body for so long.

I feel much tension in my head, but I know this release is important and will make a big difference in my life, so I persist. Finally, an affirmation comes to me, and I replace the above unhelpful thoughts and feelings with "I delight at being in my physical body, and I easily care for her with love and gratitude!" and "My support team is available to help me!" At last, I feel a deep calm and get a yes that the process is complete.

EMILY. I now open a dialogue with Joy.

JOY. I am delighted to be sharing with you, dear Emily. I am here today to say that you would do well to reframe your thinking about the word *joy*. I think you see this as being impossible and not even remotely a part of your life. You are task-driven, and that keeps joy at arm's length. I am only saying these things to be helpful. I love you very much. I am complete for this time.

EMILY. Thank you for your deep comments. I understand part of what you are saying, and I think I need to do some release work in this area. I do want to have more joy in my life. I recently felt joy starting to bubble up, but it was squashed by an unpleasant encounter with another. I love you too. Do you have more to say?

JOY. Joy has nothing to do with your everyday encounters. It is much deeper than that. Joy is a feeling of well-being no matter what is going on in the outer world. Now I am complete for this day.

EMILY. Thank you so much for this wisdom!

I am currently reading the book *True Balance* by Sonia Choquette and working through the chakra-balancing exercises. I know I will benefit from having balanced chakras. Also, I happened to buy the book *The Divine Name* by Jonathan Goldman, which includes chants for each chakra.

I get a yes to open a dialogue with Intuitive.

EMILY. Do you have comments for me?

INTUITIVE. This is exceptional. It is grand to be talking with you. You are expanding in ways you did not think were possible a few months ago. Listening to the subtle voices that come across your

215

mind is a way you connect with me. Following the hunches and feeling the vibes are ways I connect. You have been doing this all your life, but now you are doing it with awareness, and it is grand. The above chakra exercises and chants will be helpful for you to expand your receptivity. It is not just a matter of saying, "My chakras are now balanced." It is about learning how it feels to have your chakras open and balanced. This is a delightful feeling. Enjoy the exploration.

EMILY. Thank you, Intuitive, for your encouraging words of advice. Yes, I will pursue these chakra-balancing practices. I now open a dialogue with my inner children.

INNER CHILDREN. We have not given up on our color playday, as mentioned the last time we talked. We are encouraged by the deep work you did today. You released huge issues with your physical body that have been holding you back from moving forward with the use of your own personal energy. Your energy flies all over the place and is not able to help you. We close in love and smiles.

EMILY. Thank you for your helpful words. I close in love and hugs.

January 5, 2015

I had a dream on December 20, 2014, I called Wall of Water. In the dream, I was watching waves by the ocean, when suddenly, the water formed into a huge wall of water. The water crashed high up on a cliff. The energy was thrilling; then it collapsed back into its usual state. When I told others what I'd seen, they didn't believe it was possible.

I don't understand this dream and am curious to learn the meaning. I use the process for dream interpretation from the book *Unified* by Roger Lanphear. I ask my higher self for the meaning of the dream, and I hear the following:

HIGHER SELF. The wall of water is enormous knowledge from your subconscious. It will overtake much of what you thought was real. The energy is thrilling. You are not ready to live full-time in this state yet, and you have doubts that your experiences are real.

I ponder these comments. Next, I use my new release process to release emotions regarding various health issues and organs of my body.

Several days ago, I shared with some friends that I am dialoguing with aspects of myself. One friend asked if Anxious was one of my aspects. To my surprise, I could not remember. I didn't see how I could have missed that one, as being anxious is a frequent feeling of mine.

EMILY. I now open a dialogue with a possible new aspect, Anxious. Would you please speak with me today?

ANXIOUS. I am not sure. I was there yesterday when you could not remember if I was on your list or not. You could not believe you would overlook me, but you did. I am such a part of you that you do not even think of me as an aspect. I have been working with you for a long time, since early childhood, when you began to learn to be a people pleaser. I do have a positive side, which is Calm and Centered, whom you have already met. She came in first, but that is all right, as I knew you would get to me someday.

EMILY. Thank you for the explanation [see chapter 16 for Calm and Centered]. Is there anything else you would like me to know about you?

ANXIOUS. I am one of those persistent types, always in the background, but I do not mind, as I am well used in your life. Maybe someday I will be able to fully convert to Calm and Centered, but it will take some doing. Being calm and centered

217

is not going to be easy for you, but I commend you for trying. That is all I have to say at this time.

EMILY. Thank you for your comments. I now open a dialogue with my inner children.

INNER CHILDREN. We are in love with the expressive-painting book you are reading. Believe it or not, this process will be helpful in all areas of your life. It is not a diversion. Please continue in this direction.

EMILY. Thank you, dear ones. I appreciate hearing those words from you regarding my reading of *Life, Paint, and Passion* by Michele Cassou and Stewart Cubley. I am fascinated by their process of allowing a painting to express itself through one's body.

January 12, 2015

I use my new release process to release several codependent traits. One of the positive affirmations that replaces those traits is "I honor and act on my own intuitive feelings with clarity and strength." I continue until I feel better. As soon as I feel much better, I consistently get a yes that the process is complete.

EMILY. I now open a dialogue with Clarity. Are you ready to comment?

CLARITY. I am ready to speak, but please look up our last conversation.

EMILY. I just read our last and only dialogue of September 5, 2012, when you were reluctant to even join the team, as you said you did not think you could ever be clear. Please continue.

CLARITY. Yes, I did say that, and I want you to know that the word *clarity* still scares me a lot. I know you just wrote a powerful affirmation saying you would act with clarity, but well, I just don't know about being clear. This is a huge responsibility for me, and I just don't know if I am up for it. Please consider asking someone else to do this for you.

EMILY. I understand, but I just reread the other words I said to you, and you listened and agreed. I said that we are not in this alone, and we now have an even stronger support team to help. Plus, we have more aspects who are all wise and willing to be of service. And look how far you have come from your previous title, Overwhelmed and Confused. I know how you feel, but I am willing to keep saying the affirmation about acting on my own intuitive feelings with clarity and strength anyway. Is it all right if we just say the affirmation? Who knows what will happen?

CLARITY. Well, I suppose so. Saying it might even help me to be clear. All right, go ahead; keep saying the affirmation anyway.

EMILY. Thank you, Clarity. I appreciate your honesty and your effort. I love you.

I recently drew the word *self-acceptance* in a New Year's ritual. I wonder what this will mean for 2015.

EMILY. I now open a dialogue with Self-Assured.

SELF-ASSURED. I smile at the way you accepted *self-acceptance* as your word for 2015. Self-acceptance leads to being self-assured, and that is who I am. I am really a part of you. We are just beginning to become acquainted with each other. This will be a new and grand journey in self-discovery and wholeness. I appreciate your willingness to take the steps you took today so that this conversation could take place. I know I am a stretch for you, but look at all of the stretching you have been doing lately. Please keep saying the affirmations from today. I love you.

EMILY. I love you too, but the way I feel about you is the same way Clarity feels about being clear—maybe it will happen someday. Thank you for your comments.

Recently, I was meeting with some friends, and one of them shared freely about her inner child's reaction to a scary situation. I was stunned and amazed by her words.

EMILY. I now open a dialogue with my inner children.

INNER CHILDREN. We got frightened when you were with your friend—not because of the scary story she told but because you did not even notice us. You do not listen to us like she listens to her inner child. We would like to be more a part of your life. We are sad when you are sad, and we are still a bit sad even though you have cleared many issues from your energy field. We are sad at being left out.

EMILY. I am sorry. I did feel sad and afraid for you that day with my friend. I don't quite understand what happened. I have much to learn about being a parent to my own inner children. This evening, I will contact a friend, KC Hancock, who has taught expressive-arts painting. She will be able to help as I know you want to do this. Do you have more to say?

INNER CHILDREN. Not at this time. We just wanted to be acknowledged, and that has happened. You are learning, even if you don't see it. We still love you!

EMILY. I love you too.

January 19, 2015

I use my new release process to release codependent traits and replace them with strong, positive affirmations. A new trait to release is the fear of authority figures, which I replace with the affirmation "I am at ease and confident around persons in authority roles."

I now use my new release process to release emotions regarding various health issues and organs of my body. As soon as I feel better, I check, and the issue is always released.

I cannot prove any of this is real, but my body likes the results, and I feel better, so I continue.

A part of my morning routine is to send love and gratitude to my body's cells. It recently came to me to ask for and feel God's love in my cells.

EMILY. I am now ready to dialogue with Beloved. Do you have comments?

BELOVED. My dear Emily, please do not ever think you are unloved. There is so much love for you here in the unseen world that you cannot begin to imagine from your small world view. Please sit, and let these words soak into your being. Feel the love, and allow it to permeate every part of you. You are making a good start with the addition of feeling God's love vibrating in your cells each morning. I close in love and light.

EMILY. Thank you so much, Beloved, for your encouraging words. I now open a dialogue with Intuitive.

INTUITIVE. I am a small, subtle voice that takes much attunement to hear or notice. You do well here in the sheltered environment of your special dialogue day. In the outside world, things are different. Whenever you are not sure if I am speaking, go to a quiet place by yourself, and ask again. Then you can really hear. And please do not be hard on yourself when you have a negative experience, as such experiences can be most worthwhile.

EMILY. Thank you for the advice. I was recently overwhelmed with a negative experience and did not know what to do. Now I can picture this happening differently. I am now ready to open a dialogue with Strength.

STRENGTH. Oh, this is fun. It has been a long time since we spoke. I would like to comment on your tenacity at staying with your feelings despite your labeling some of them as negative feelings. This is a path of strength, integrity, and authenticity.

EMILY. Thank you, Strength, for the encouragement. I feel a strong urge these days to allow negative feelings to be released from my body. I now open a dialogue with my inner children.

INNER CHILDREN. We feel much better this day, especially after you took our advice and set up a date to do the expressive painting. We are also looking forward to our next Silver Falls retreat. Those are always fun and exciting. We close in love and smiles.

EMILY. I am glad you are feeling better. I love you all.

Chapter 19

My Own Body Is
Someone for Me to Love

January 25, 2015, Silver Falls Retreat, Day 1

I AM EXCITED AS I begin this adventure into the unseen world with another personal retreat to a small heated cabin in Silver Falls State Park. Armed with warm clothes, I settle in to enjoy the exploration. I can never guess what will happen. It is guaranteed to be a surprise.

I begin the evening with first chakra work. It is calming and strengthening.

I have been doing everything Bradshaw mentions in his book *Homecoming* to avoid health issues. One suggestion is that we get the nurturing we need from other adults. Despite many nurturing friends who have volunteered to assist, this is not working for me in a parenting role. Suddenly, I have the following thought: *I am getting my nurturing from my connections in the unseen world.*

Then I wonder what my inner children would say about parenting. I immediately hear that I would benefit from reclaiming and welcoming the ancient wise woman part of myself.

This idea surprises me, but I have come to trust what my aspects tell me. I will explore this later in my retreat.

Then I get a yes that all the release work and dialogues I have been doing are helping me to transform myself. It seems I have been doing inner-child work all along, just my own unique version.

January 26, 2015, Silver Falls Retreat, Day 2

I begin with second chakra material from Sonia Choquette's book *True Balance*. Sonia says the second chakra is the domain of the inner child and that a two-year-old can't get enough of life. This is unsettling for me, as my two-and-a-half-year-old self almost checked out of life.

Then I find another statement: "I have the right to enjoy my inner child and take delight in life." I find myself laughing at this wonderful synchronicity and feeling joy bubble up inside my body. I can enjoy my own inner child at any age.

I get a yes to ask for interpretation of two dreams. Dreams are playing a vital role in my life these days. They seem to mirror what is happening in my waking life and suggest new pathways for me to follow. With curiosity, I proceed.

Using the process from the book *Unified* by Roger Lanphear, I ask my higher self for the meaning of a dream from January 8, 2015, called Amicable Divorce, in which I watched a Santa Claus in the sky. Then I saw a man and a woman dividing up their belongings. All was going well, except the woman looked worried after she learned her monthly income would be less than anticipated. Then I drove away, puzzled as to why such nice people were getting a divorce. I learn this dream means the following:

HIGHER SELF. You see old beliefs and know they are made up. You are sorting through old beliefs to see which to keep and which to leave. You do this without anxiety, but you are not quite trusting of the process and fear some loss. Then you proceed through old beliefs in the unconscious. You are able to release the ones that don't serve you.

This puzzling dream turns out to be reassuring when I hear its meaning from my higher self. I have recently been releasing many things that no longer serve me: false beliefs, codependent traits, and unhelpful thoughts.

My next dream was Family Gathering from January 12, 2015. In it, I was with a group of people around a large table. We were all eating, but there was much partially eaten food. More food kept appearing. One man I didn't recognize had to leave due to problems with his work crew. He looked and acted oddly. I learn this dream means the following:

HIGHER SELF. You see your connections with other parts of yourself, and you wish to connect with these parts. Your parts are trying to nourish you, but they are only partially successful. They keep trying anyway. One of your parts does things differently, and this shocks you. You disown some parts as not being part of you.

This dream was also puzzling until I heard the interpretation. Now I relax about the message.

I get a yes that it is time to continue acknowledgment and integration of my aspects. I began the process at my last Silver Falls retreat on October 29, 2014 (see chapter 16), but I did not have time to finish.

Once again, there is no how-to book for what I am doing. I proceed as guided by my aspects on this amazing path. With a tight throat, I continue, knowing I might hear a message from some and feel a message from others.

Here is the result as I acknowledge, visualize, and integrate with all but one of my remaining aspects:

ACKNOWLEDGMENT OF ASPECTS

I hear nothing from Strength.

My shoulders drop, and I feel as if I am sinking into my body. I feel completely grounded and strong. I know Strength is a part of the team.

ACCEPTANCE. Did you not write *self-acceptance* as your word for 2015?

I smile and know Acceptance is a part of the team.

PLAYFUL. Oh, the fun we are going to have together when you fully integrate with me! And look at all the fun you are having today. It has already begun!

I hear laughter, and I know Playful is a part of the team.

FEAR AND TAKES ACTION AND CONNECTED TO SOURCE. Fear is a feeling that needs to be allowed to move through your body and is not an aspect. Takes Action and Connected to Source are specific actions you can take, but they are not aspects.

I remove Fear, Takes Action, and Connected to Source from my list. I find this amazing, as fear has been intense for me in my life, but I have come to trust my guidance. This does not mean I will never be afraid, just that fear is not an aspect.

ABILITY TO SAY NO. I am with you even as you learn to utilize my part.

INTEGRITY. I came through the feeling of anger, but I am one of your aspects—an important one.

GUIDED. I am still new for you, but I am certainly an aspect. You are still releasing my old role of People Pleaser, but that will pass. I suggest you do a release process on that trait.

I make a note to do this in the future.

ADVENTUROUS. Well, I am sure you have no doubt that you and I are fully integrated and have been for much of your life.

COMPASSION. I recently expanded to include compassion for others as well as for yourself. I am new for you, but as you continue with your current processes, I will become more real, and you will be able to accept me, for I am one of your aspects.

TRUST AND FAITH IN SELF. You know we are growing like a seed inside of you. Someday we will sprout into full bloom. We are one aspect: Trust and Faith in Self.

CREATIVE. You are coming along just fine!

I hear nothing from Powerful.
My shoulders drop, and I feel a strength in the core of my being. I know this is an aspect, even if it is not yet integrated.

TRUST AND FAITH IN GUIDANCE. We are different from Guided, as we are how you are really able to utilize your gift of guidance. Yes, we are one of your aspects.

EMILY. I am grateful and honored to have each one of you on the team. Welcome!

This is the end of my list of aspects. I am concerned I might have missed one, as something about wisdom keeps coming to me. I wonder if Wise is one of my aspects, and I hear, "Wise is who you are already. There is nothing you have to do to become wise. When you work with all of the above aspects, you will learn this. There are many wonderful traits you could list, but the aspects you now have on your list are the missing ones you needed to acknowledge."

I feel complete with this phase of my process. I have a knowing that as my aspects integrate, they bring wholeness.

I now get a yes that I need to do a ceremony to give value to each aspect and forgive myself for separating from them, even though it might have happened at a young age. Once again, there is no how-to book, so I proceed as guided by my aspects. Here is the result:

CEREMONY IN RECOGNITION OF THE VALUE OF MY ASPECTS

Each and every aspect is hereby recognized
as being of the utmost value to me.
I honor and thank you all for returning
to me and for your integration.
I love you all.
I ask your forgiveness for disowning you years ago.
You all are of extreme value to me. If you still wish to continue
with me, please allow me to add your name on this page.

MY VALUED ASPECTS

Tenacity   Courage
Flexible   Balanced   Calm and Centered
Beloved   Precious   Clarity   Organized
Self-Assured   Safety Team and Security Force
Intuitive   Joy   Strength   Acceptance
Playful   Ability to Say No   Integrity
Guided   Adventurous   Creative
Compassion   Trust and Faith in Self
Powerful   Trust and Faith in Guidance

I honor each of you with love!

I sing "Amen" and dance around the room. I say, "Yes!" to life. I do a self-forgiveness process around separating from my aspects. As I close this day, I am filled with deep peace.

January 27, 2015, Silver Falls Retreat, Day 3

I begin this day by working with Sonia Choquette's chakra material from *True Balance* for first, second, and third chakras.

I get a yes to once again release my inability to say no. As I begin, I have the thought to release the belief that if I say no, I will not be loved. I use my new release process and replace that unhelpful belief with the affirmations "I have the right to say no. God, my higher self, and my support team all love me no matter what" and "I love and approve of myself no matter what."

I become stalled in the process. On a hunch, I ask and get a yes that I need to once again use the paper and pastels to say no. I follow this suggestion, and during the process, I receive more clarity regarding my inability to say no. I burn the paper.

EMILY. I now open a dialogue with Clarity. Please comment.

CLARITY. I am pleased I stayed with the team. I really think I can help you and make a difference in your life. Thank you for believing in me even when I doubted. I love you no matter what!

EMILY. Thank you so much, Clarity. You are precious to me, and I thank you for believing in me. I love you too no matter what! I now open a dialogue with People Pleaser.

PEOPLE PLEASER. It has been a while, but I am still around. You are doing a great job of moving past my negative side, and the more you connect with the higher energies, the less you will see of me. This is good.

EMILY. Thank you. I am pleased. I now open a dialogue with Precious.

PRECIOUS. I know you still do not really think we, your aspects, are real, but I love that you show up for these wonderful talks. What makes you think you are not worthy of having conversations with the unseen world? It is time for you to release all blocks to believing that these are real talks, for they are real talks.

EMILY. I know you are correct. I don't know why I doubt, but on some level, I do feel unworthy. Who am I to be having these conversations?

PRECIOUS. Just let me love you for a few minutes, and then say out loud how worthy you really are. Go ahead. Try it.

I pause to see if I can feel anything and am amazed as I feel a warm blanket of love being tucked around my body. I say the following aloud:

EMILY. I am worthy of having these conversations!

Then I get a yes that Powerful wishes to dialogue with me. I force myself to continue.

EMILY. I now open a dialogue with Powerful. Do you have comments?

POWERFUL. Yes, I wish to talk with you at this time. I am the one you are most afraid of on your entire list of aspects, yet here I am on your list. That should be a clue in itself. Yes, you are a powerful person who came here to Earth to redo some things. I suggest you just sit with me by your side every so often. Get used to my being near you. You do not have to take my energy inside yourself at this time.

EMILY. That sounds like something I can do. Thank you for your suggestion. I now open a dialogue with my inner children.

INNER CHILDREN. We think it would be good for you to do the grieving suggestion from John Bradshaw's book *Homecoming* so you can finally get over your childhood and start to enjoy all the wonderful things you are now doing. You know you chose the right and perfect childhood for what you wanted to accomplish in this life. We suggest you pick out the things you feel would be helpful from Bradshaw and skip the rest. We see you wanting to do it all perfectly, and we wish you would scrap that idea. We love you. Time to go.

EMILY. Thanks for the great hints. I love you all.

Following the suggestion from my inner children, I use Bradshaw's material to grieve the loss of a normal childhood. I feel much relief as I do the process. I come to realize that a normal childhood would not have prepared me to be who I am today, and I would have missed these incredible experiences.

Then I have the idea that I need to acknowledge the contribution of the shadow side for each of my aspects. I get a yes that this would be helpful. Again, there is no how-to book to follow. My intuition leads me to respectfully connect with the original title for each aspect. Here is the result:

ACKNOWLEDGMENT CEREMONY
FOR MY ORIGINAL ASPECTS

Rigid Taskmaster and Stern Enforcer helped me get things done.
Saboteur, Sick Patient in Hospital (Self-Esteem), Snit and
Snat, and Black Woman helped me learn from my dreams.
Overwhelmed and Confused gave me an
out when I didn't know what to do.
Defective helped me learn that some old
family patterns are not true.
Unlovable helped me learn I am loved.
Unworthy helped me learn I am worthy.
Safety Team and Security Force protected me.
Super-Responsible One, Perfectionist, and People Pleaser helped
me to cope with my childhood and assisted with my career.
Sadness, Inadequate, and Pity gave me ways to
allow myself to cry and release feelings.
Shy One gave me a great cover-up role to cope with my early years.
Fear and Anger helped me identify and release feelings.
Inability to Say No helped me stay invisible.
High Judge gave me some rules to live by.
Creative, Powerful, and Trust and Faith in Guidance
had no other original names but were given to me
intuitively, which helped me believe in my intuition.
Anxious helped me to identify when something was off.
I now realize how much each of you did for me, and I want
you to know that I love you, honor you, and appreciate you.
Thank you!

I get a yes to follow up on the suggestion my inner children made on day one of this retreat. At that time, my inner children told me I would benefit from reclaiming and welcoming the ancient wise woman part of myself.

I review Bradshaw's *Homecoming*, in which he suggests the inner child needs a wise adult parental figure. His parental figure looks like a powerful wizard. I am having trouble with this, as I do not feel I have an ancient wise-woman part.

Then I get the idea to use my new release process to release doubts that I have an ancient wise-woman part and replace those unhelpful thoughts with the affirmation "I welcome back the ancient wise-woman part of me with open arms and an open heart." I stay with this process until I feel better. Then I know that I do have an ancient wise woman to assist me in my life. I feel honored and blessed as I close another amazing day.

January 28, 2015, Silver Falls Retreat, Day 4

I awake with a surprise realization that my own body is actually someone for me to love. I have never thought of my body this way before. I am being prompted to open my heart to love, and now I am being given a safe place to begin: my own body.

Now that I am ready to believe that I do have an ancient wise-woman part, I am ready to complete the welcome ceremony for my inner children. This brings my inner-child work to completion. The words of this ceremony flow effortlessly through my being.

WELCOME CEREMONY

Welcome back,
Ancient Wise Woman,
Two-and-a-half-year-old Little Emily, and
Inner Children.
My heart has longed for all of you for many years,
but I did not know what that longing was.
My body has longed for all of you for many years,
but I did not know what that longing was.
My spirit has longed for all of you for many years,
but I did not know what that longing was.
My soul has longed for all of you for many years,
but I did not know what that longing was.
I welcome all of you into my heart, my
body, my spirit, and my soul.
Welcome home!

I find myself sitting in a place of deep peace.

EMILY. I open a dialogue with Calm and Centered.

CALM AND CENTERED. Can you really feel how you feel right now? Well, that is a great example of my presence. You will feel this way much more now that we have integrated. Blessings on the rest of your life. I close for now, and I thank you for the wonderful ceremonies.

EMILY. I do feel calm and centered and somehow different in my body. I open a dialogue with Ancient Wise Woman.

ANCIENT WISE WOMAN. Didn't think I was real, did you? Well, I am, and I am alive and well. I am glad to be with you at last. It is an honor. I look forward to our explorations together. Go in peace this day. Feel the love from the trees, the growing green plants, your body, and so much more.

EMILY. I am honored to have you with me on my journey. Thank you for making yourself known. I love you. I open a dialogue with my inner children.

INNER CHILDREN. We loved the wonderful welcome ceremony and the expansion of your heart toward all of us. We close in giggles and laughter.

EMILY. Thank you. I love you all. I close another amazing retreat!

Chart of Aspects as of January 28, 2015

New Name	Previous Name	Date First Noted	Date Fully Integrated
Tenacity	Rigid Taskmaster	4-7-12	5-8-12
Courage	Stern Enforcer	4-7-12	5-8-12
Flexible	Saboteur	6-4-12	1-22-13
Balanced	Defective	6-12-12	8-11-12
Calm and Centered	Anxious	10-29-14	10-29-14
Beloved	Unlovable	6-12-12	9-10-12
Precious	Unworthy	6-12-12	11-6-12
Clarity	Overwhelmed and Confused	6-20-12	9-5-12
Organized	Perfectionist	7-9-12	8-13-12
Self-Assured	Sick Hospital Patient Self-Esteem	7-25-12 10-3-12	10-3-12
Safety Team and Security Force	Safety Team and Security Force	8-3-12	8-3-12
Intuitive	Super-Responsible One	8-6-12	8-6-12
Joy	Sadness	8-6-12	8-6-12
Strength	Inadequate	8-11-12	8-11-12
Acceptance	Pity	8-27-12	9-5-12

Playful	Shy One	8-27-12	8-27-12
Ability to Say No	Inability to Say No	9-11-12	5-18-13
Integrity	Anger	9-11-12	9-11-12
Guided	People Pleaser	9-12-12	7-22-13
Adventurous	Snit and Snat	9-21-12	11-6-12
Compassion	High Judge	11-19-12	11-19-12
Trust and Faith in Self	Black Woman in Dream	12-12-12	5-5-14
Creative	Creative	1-23-13	1-23-13
Powerful	Powerful	12-2-13	
Trust and Faith in Guidance	Trust and Faith in Guidance	5-5-14	5-26-14

Chapter 20

Wholeness of Being

February 2, 2015

I AM BETWEEN SLEEPING and waking when I have the thought that I do not know how to parent or even love my own inner children. Then I hear three amazing messages:

INNER CHILDREN. You are not our parent; we are a part of you. When you love yourself, you love us.

HIGHER SELF. Do not worry so. Enjoy the ride!

INNER CHILDREN. You do not need to parent us. You only need to allow your higher self to parent you. See how you are already being given great information and being loved unconditionally by your higher self. Now all you have to do is love back. We love you.

EMILY. I hardly know what to say. Thank you for the advice. I love you too. Rather, I love myself, which includes you!

I hear laughter.

February 6, 2015

I explore expressive painting and find it fascinating. First, I hold my brush over a muffin tin with a variety of tempera paint colors and wait to see where my hand will be directed. I am drawn to specific colors, and gradually, a painting emerges—and then another.

My first is a series of expanding circles from pinks and reds in the center out into rings of yellows and then into purples. My hand is directed to put a black area in one corner of the painting.

My second is an energetic green woman with a mass of yellow-and-red hair standing straight out all over her head. She casts off blobs of blue with one hand as she dances over two rainbows.

This experience is exciting and fills me with a sense of freedom. Despite having no idea what this is all about, I feel a deep inner peace.

February 9, 2015

I call in my support team and use my new release process to release doubts that what I hear is true and replace those unhelpful thoughts with the affirmation "I completely trust that what I hear is accurate and worthy of note." Then I release the thought that what I am doing is risky business and replace it with "I am completely safe and supported by the universe." Releasing takes a while each time, but when I feel relief, I know the process is complete.

EMILY. I now open a dialogue with Compassion.

COMPASSION. I am ready to talk with you. Please feel my presence as you relax and drop into surrender. Yes, that's it. Your compassion is needed for your dear self. Acceptance is close, but it is not the same. True compassion includes acceptance. I suggest you sit with these ideas and just let them settle into your being. Then see what happens. I close in love and compassion.

EMILY. Thank you for your comments. I will act on these suggestions. I now open a dialogue with my inner children.

INNER CHILDREN. We are thrilled with the expressive painting you did on Friday. It was marvelous and exciting! Please hold dialogues with the images you created that day. You will be surprised. This is how you get to know us better too. We see you doubting some of your inner-child work. There is no need for this. Follow our suggestions and your own intuition, and go from there. Hunches and guidance will be given for your highest and best. We close for now in delight and joy. We wish you could feel some of our delight and joy at least every so often. We love you.

EMILY. Thank you! I have read that an adult cannot trust the guidance of an inner child, but you all seem wise to me. Do you have any comments?

INNER CHILDREN. Of course you can trust us. We are a part of you. We are not some silly character; we are wise beyond belief. We are a part of your ancient wise one, and we are here to help you. We are your own inner children who are a part of you. This might not all make sense at this time, but please do not erase these words.

EMILY. All right. Thank you. I love you. I now open a dialogue with Creative.

CREATIVE. We have hardly ever spoken. I am quiet, but I am here, and I would like to suggest that you recognize me more as an aspect of yourself. You are extremely creative but not in a way to be making up all of these dialogues. You really are having dialogues with parts of yourself. I am pleased as well with the expressive painting, but I would like you to see that you are creative in many other ways besides art. Almost everything you do is creative. I am referring to your change in attitude toward all you do. These are your acts of creativity, and you will feel much pleasure in thinking of yourself as a creative person. I close for today with love and encouragement.

EMILY. Yes, you are very encouraging. I will sit with this. I love you too.

February 16, 2015

More than a year ago, when I was preparing for the Inner-Team workshop (see chapter 11), I asked each aspect for permission to share our conversations. Not all said yes, and I included only those who gave permission in the workshop. Today the nudge to share my dialogues with others is so strong that I again ask for permission from the three aspects who were not willing the first time.

EMILY. I now open a dialogue with Overwhelmed and Confused.

OVERWHELMED AND CONFUSED. Oh, I don't like to be put in the spotlight. I know you want to share my words with others, but well, I don't know if I like this or not.

EMILY. Yes, you are correct that I wish to share your words with others. I would like it if you could consider this an honor. What we have done together is wonderful and will be able to help others see that they have aspects just as I do. You were one of the first to appear, and I would like to include you in my future sharing. Are you all right with this? I will always speak of you with great respect.

OVERWHELMED AND CONFUSED. I know you always speak of me with respect. In fact, you respect all of us. I just feel inadequate—that's all.

242

EMILY. Yes, I know. You are a vulnerable one, and that is what makes you extremely important to my story. It could not be told well without you. Does this help?

OVERWHELMED AND CONFUSED. Well, yes, it does. I guess it is all right to share my words with others after all.

EMILY. I am glad to hear this. Thank you so much for your honesty and for sharing your concern. This is a step toward open communication and a valuable tool you are helping me to learn. Thank you again. I now open a dialogue with Flexible.

FLEXIBLE. I now see the value of what you will be doing.

EMILY. I am relieved to hear this. You were also one of my first contacts, and you are unique. Please allow me to include you in my sharing with others.

FLEXIBLE. Yes, please share my story along with the rest. I think there is more flexibility in your body these days too now that yoga has been included in your life. I am really enjoying the feeling that yoga brings.

EMILY. Thank you, Flexible. I now open a dialogue with High Judge.

HIGH JUDGE. You did not expect to need to talk to me again, did you? Well, I am still here, and you can see me in all of the releases of judgments you are being led to do. This releasing will really help you in the long run. You have spent much of your life closely linked to me, so this is a huge break from old patterns you are breaking down. Please continue with the releases, and do not get discouraged. Someday you will be able to accept yourself and all others just the way you are and just the way they are.

EMILY. Thank you for your helpful words. May I include you in the sharing of our story?

HIGH JUDGE. Of course you may. I am an important part as well.

EMILY. Yes, you are important. Thank you again.

After receiving the above permissions, I continue with my dialogues.

EMILY. I now open a dialogue with Compassion.

COMPASSION. I am more of the quiet side of the story, but I will grow as you grow. Right now, I am quite small from disuse, but I am growing, and one day I will be in full bloom. I come from the heart. As you open your heart, I will be more evident in your life. I close in love and compassion for your dear self.

EMILY. Thank you for the kind words. I now open a dialogue with my inner children.

INNER CHILDREN. Oh, the expressive painting was grand! We would like it if you would do a quick dialogue with each painting before you close today. And we can't wait to be shared with others. What we are doing is unique and noteworthy. Please set a date to do more painting. We all look forward to our trip next week, especially since you will be with your friend who really knows how to play. We have no more to say today. Love and kisses.

EMILY. I will ponder this idea of doing more expressive painting. For now, I will see if it's possible to actually dialogue with an expressive painting, as you suggest.

Who ever thought of holding a conversation with a painting? However, I have come to trust my guidance and will see what happens. After all, these paintings are my creations, so maybe they are no different from my aspects. I decide to give this a try.

EMILY. I now open a dialogue with my first painting. Do you have something to share?

COLORED CIRCLES WITH DARK SPOT. Go deep inside where I reside. I am that part of you that has fear despite the existence of joy and love. See how the love and joy (yellows and purples) enclose and protect the heart, the core of you (pinks and reds), from the fear (black spot)? You are always safe from the fear, but you might want to ask it to leave, as it no longer serves you. Thank you for asking me this day.

EMILY. Incredible! I appreciate this amazing wisdom. I will also follow your suggestion about the fear part. I now open a dialogue with my second painting. Do you have something to share?

GREEN GIRL WHO DANCES ON RAINBOWS. See how I am releasing the blobs? See how free I am? This freedom is deep inside of you, yearning to be released. I am your release process. I love what I am doing. I love being me. Thank you for asking.

EMILY. Amazing! Thank you for this confirmation of all the release processing I have been doing. I am overjoyed to learn that this is so beneficial. I thank each of you for these insights and words of wisdom. I close in love and appreciation for both of you.

It seems our inner selves truly wish to enlighten us, even when they come through in the form of art.

Weeks Later

I do a release process on fear, as my first expressive painting suggested, and I feel relief as fear melts away.

The urge to share these dialogues with others continues to grow. Since most were handwritten, I am keying them into a file on my laptop. Doing this has made me realize I haven't fully integrated with my aspect Powerful. The thought of myself as a powerful person still makes me uneasy. An energy practitioner is helping me to accept the idea of being powerful, and although that acceptance is not coming easily, I am making progress.

I attend a Tom Kenyon sound-healing event in Seattle, during which we are led in several deep meditations. While in one of the meditations, Powerful comes forth with the message "I am ready for integration."

A Few Days Later

I connect with my support team and ponder the words from Powerful. It seems I must finally acknowledge that Powerful is one of my aspects. Then I remember a previous message from this aspect: I am the one who chooses when it is time for integration. As with many of my other aspects, this one doesn't have to be perfected before integration. Willingness is the only requirement. With unease in the pit of my stomach, I hold a simple candle celebration to welcome Powerful to the team.

EMILY. Do you have any words for me, Powerful?

POWERFUL. Indeed I do. I am in honor of all you have done to reach this step. I realize you do not really see yourself as the powerful individual you are, but you are willing to proceed with life regardless. Willingness is the first step. Thank you, and blessings on this day. I close in love and power, for love is the only real power in the universe. Good day.

EMILY. My heart overflows with gratitude. Thank you!

Today

The dialogues with unseen parts of myself are an ongoing adventure. Every one rewards me with the discovery of something new and incredible. It is like a surprise party; I never know who will speak or what I will hear.

My aspects continue to give me astonishing wisdom, honest feedback, and practical advice. I follow their suggestions out of trust in the wisdom of my inner world.

The entire experience is enormously transformative. I am a completely different person than I was a few short years ago, when I had no idea about inner guidance. Now I cannot imagine my life without this part of myself.

Another difference is that my circle of friends has changed. I used to be in awe of people who could do astounding things, and I felt intimidated. Now some of these strong leaders and powerful energy workers are my friends.

I have long since released my major fear, the health challenges that initiated this adventure, and I am healthy, but if an issue arises, I have strong inner guidance and a large toolbox of resources to deal with it.

I am no longer afraid to acknowledge the presence of negative issues in my life. Thanks to my aspects, who gave me a number of simple, effective ways to release obsolete beliefs, thoughts, and emotions, I know what to do when I encounter an uncomfortable situation. This knowledge lets my body, mind, and spirit be fully alive, something I longed for my entire life.

That longing was a vague sense that something was lacking, but I could not identify what it was. Now that I am connected with my aspects, that sense of lacking is gone. As I integrated them, I moved into a wholeness of being that I previously couldn't have imagined.

The quest for this fulfillment is joy-filled, amazing, distressing, loving, and disrupting and pushes me to grow and be more than I ever thought possible, and it is not complete. I have a feeling it will never end. Learning is a lifelong journey, and I will leave no stone unturned in my search for more wisdom.

As you explore your inner unseen world, you will discover aspects of yourself that will transform your life. See appendix D for guidance on discovering your inner world.

Enjoy your adventure!

How to Get Yes-or-No Answers to Your Questions

A. **Be grounded.** Being grounded helps you focus in your body. There are many methods, but they all consist of connecting with the earth. Some suggestions include the following: visualize your feet sending roots into the ground, hold a crystal and command your energy to connect with the ground, or feel a cord going from your spine into the ground. (Also, see *Trust Your Vibes* by Sonia Choquette.)

B. **Choose a method to get yes-or-no answers.** Suggestions include the following: pendulum, kinesiology, or muscle testing. These are well described online. Choose one that works for you. Some suggested sites are as follows:

- Pendulum: "Letter to Robin: A Mini-Course in Pendulum Dowsing" by Walt Woods at www.lettertorobin. wordpress.com

- Kinesiology: "PKTT Kinesiology Testing" by Perelandra Center for Nature Research at www.perelandra-ltd.com
- Muscle Testing: "Healing with EFT" at www.healing-with-eft.com/self-muscle-testing

C. **Check to be sure you are in polarity.** When you are in polarity, your body's energy is flowing in a beneficial direction.

- To check your polarity, ask an obvious yes question and an obvious no question using your chosen method from above.
- If you get the correct answer, continue with step D.
- If you do not get the correct answer, your energy flow may be reversed. To remedy this, gently tap your thymus gland (the middle of your chest) and visualize your energy going up the back side of your body, over the top of your head, and down the front of your body. Do this about three times, and check again. Continue this process until you get correct yes-and-no answers for your statements. (Also, see *Spring Forest Qigong, Level One for Health* by Master Chunyi Lin or *Barefoot Doctor's Guide to the Tao* by Stephen Russell.)

D. **Practice your yes-and-no method.** Now you are ready to ask questions. Start with obvious yes-and-no statements until you feel confident in your abilities. Then venture into asking your own questions. Your body knows the correct answers; you are now developing confidence in this wisdom.

Appendix B

Release and Affirmation Examples

- Release the fear of angry people, and replace it with "I am completely at ease with angry people. I know it is their stuff and not mine" (June 9, 2014).
- Release the assumption of responsibility for the feelings and behavior of others, and replace it with "I allow all others to have their own feelings and behavior with no impact upon myself" (June 2, 2014).
- Release the fear of disapproval and rejection by others, and replace it with "I love and approve of myself just the way I am" (June 2, 2014).
- Release the craving for validation of self-worth from others, and replace it with "I completely love and approve of myself. I know I am completely worthy of God's love, my own love, and all love" (May 26, 2014).
- Release harsh self-judgment, and replace it with "I completely love and accept myself" (July 7, 2014).

- Release the fear to trust due to lack of trust in self, and replace it with "I completely trust myself, and I completely trust life" (July 7, 2014).
- Release the feeling that discovery of the real self will cause rejection, and replace it with "I now feel completely sure of myself and my actions" (August 4, 2014).
- Release the fear of criticism and judgment despite the tendency to be critical and judgmental of others, and replace it with "I completely accept myself and others just the way we are" (September 8, 2014).
- Release the fear of trusting the universe for support, and replace it with "I completely trust the universe to support me" (September 8, 2014).

The wording is based on books by Karol Truman and Louise Hay, with revisions of my own.

New Release Process

1. **Visualize divine light in, around, and through your body.**
2. **Choose your support team, and ask them to connect with you.** Select only spiritual figures you highly respect. Some suggestions might include your own higher self, Jesus, Buddha, Quan Yin, the archangels, or your own guardian angel.
3. **Decide what you want to release.** Choose an issue that no longer serves you, and open your mind to your feelings and thoughts connected with the issue. For example, "I fear disapproval and rejection by others." (Also, see the lists found in *Feelings Buried Alive Never Die* by Karol Truman and *You Can Heal Your Life* by Louise Hay.)
4. **Identify a positive affirmation to replace what you are releasing.** Open your heart and mind to a new positive affirmation that will replace what you are releasing. Trust that the perfect one will come into your mind. Affirmation examples might include the following: "I trust my intuitive self. I trust my higher self. I love myself just the way I am." (Also, see affirmations in the above books.)

5. **Ask your support team to help you release these feelings and thoughts and replace them with your new positive affirmation while making simple body movements.** Repeat your request while gently tapping your chest (the thymus gland) with one hand, rocking back and forth, and making the infinity symbol (a figure eight on its side) with your other hand. For example, say the following:

I ask my support team to please help me release my fear of disapproval and rejection by others and replace it with the affirmation "I trust my intuitive self. I trust my higher self. I love myself just the way I am." At the same time, I gently tap my chest with my left hand, rock back and forth, and make the infinity symbol in the air with my right hand.

6. **Allow the process to happen.** Continue to repeat your request along with the body movements. It will take as long as it takes, but usually, five to ten minutes is sufficient.
7. **Physical sensations.** With some issues, you might feel physical sensations as energy is moving in your body. For example, I often feel some tension in my throat or my head. I've found this to be normal, and the tensions always pass quickly as I continue the process.
8. **Feeling better.** At some point, you will feel much better. This means the process is complete. For example, I usually start to feel better after about three to five minutes. Then my whole body relaxes, and I feel much better. Then I know the process is complete. (Also, see appendix A for information on how to get answers to yes-or-no questions.)
9. **Thank your support team for their assistance.**

Guidance for Discovering Your Inner World

1. Sit quietly with pen and paper or your computer.
2. Visualize divine light in, around, and through your body.
3. **Choose your support team.** Select only spiritual figures you highly respect. Some suggestions might include your own higher self, Jesus, Buddha, Quan Yin, the archangels, or your own guardian angel.
4. **Connect with your support team.** Simply ask each one to be present at this time and stay with you until you have completed your dialogue session.
5. **Ask for one of your aspects to come forth.** You will feel, hear, or sense who would like to dialogue with you. Then simply allow the words to flow. Remember, this is a part of your own self you are connecting with, so this part will have only your highest good as a goal. Your aspect's words

will be honest and might be difficult to accept, but that is their worth.

6. **Write or key the words you are given.** Much wisdom can come from your aspects or parts of yourself. Try not to judge where the information is coming from or whether or not it is true. Just let the words flow. You might be surprised as you read your notes after the session.

7. **Enjoy a whole new dimension to your life.** You now have a tool for communication with your aspects, your body, your feelings, your dream images, your higher self, your support team, and even your expressive paintings.

Note: The above process is complete as stated. If you wish to get yes-or-no answers to your questions, see appendix A. This is not necessary, however, to have meaningful dialogues with your aspects.

Reference List

Bradshaw, John. *Homecoming: Reclaiming and Championing Your Inner Child.* New York, NY: Bantam Press, 1990.

Cassou, Michele, and Stewart Cubley. *Life, Paint, and Passion.* New York, NY: Tarcher/Penguin, 1995.

Choquette, Sonia. www.soniachoquette.com.

Grieco, Mary Hayes. *Unconditional Forgiveness.* New York, NY: Atria Books and Hillsboro, OR: Beyond Words, 2011.

Hancock, KC. Expressive Arts. www.kchancock.com.

Haner, Jean. www.jeanhaner.com.

Hay, Louise. *You Can Heal Your Life.* Carlsbad, CA: Hay House Inc., 1987.

Hicks, Esther, and Jerry Hicks. *Ask and It Is Given.* Carlsbad, CA: Hay House, Inc., 2004.

Hoefler, Michael. Energy Empowerment and Dowser, Montana, www.facebook.com.

Kenyon, Tom. Sound Healer. www.tomkenyon.com.

Lanphear, Roger G. *Spirituality of the Third Millennium*. Indianapolis, IN: Dog Ear Publishing, 2010.

Lanphear, Roger G. *Unified*. Marina del Rey, CA: DeVorss & Co., 1987.

O'Neill, Karen. www.massagetherapy.com/get-a-massage/kareno'neill

Richardson, Georgie. Unity Minister (Retired) and Spiritual Counselor.

Spring Forest Qigong. www.springforestqigong.com.

Truman, Karol. *Feelings Buried Alive Never Die*. Las Vegas, NV: Olympus Distributing, 1991.

Wevers, Mary Jo. Jungian Karmic Astrologer. www.maryjowevers.com.

Index

About the Author

EMILY WELLS IS A retired college professor of health information management. A medical wake-up call led her to an astonishing journey of self-discovery and self-empowerment. This journey transformed her life.

She teaches Spring Forest Qigong and enjoys visiting her daughters and grandchildren, reading, hiking, bicycle riding, traveling, and gardening. She and her husband live in western Oregon.

CPSIA information can be obtained
at www.ICGtesting.com
Printed in the USA
FSHW011952100519
58051FS